Cambridge Elements

Elements in Experimental Political Science
edited by
James N. Druckman
University of Rochester

ELITISM VERSUS POPULISM

Experiments on the Dual Threat to American Democracy

Curtis Bram
The University of Texas at Dallas

Shaftesbury Road, Cambridge CB2 8EA, United Kingdom

One Liberty Plaza, 20th Floor, New York, NY 10006, USA

477 Williamstown Road, Port Melbourne, VIC 3207, Australia

314–321, 3rd Floor, Plot 3, Splendor Forum, Jasola District Centre, New Delhi – 110025, India

103 Penang Road, #05–06/07, Visioncrest Commercial, Singapore 238467

Cambridge University Press is part of Cambridge University Press & Assessment, a department of the University of Cambridge.

We share the University's mission to contribute to society through the pursuit of education, learning and research at the highest international levels of excellence.

www.cambridge.org
Information on this title: www.cambridge.org/9781009546935

DOI: 10.1017/9781009546898

First published 2025

A catalogue record for this publication is available from the British Library

ISBN 978-1-009-54693-5 Hardback
ISBN 978-1-009-54694-2 Paperback
ISSN 2633-3368 (online)
ISSN 2633-335X (print)

Additional resources for this publication at www.cambridge.org/bram

Elitism versus Populism

Experiments on the Dual Threat to American Democracy

Elements in Experimental Political Science

DOI: 10.1017/9781009546898
First published online: May 2025

Curtis Bram
The University of Texas at Dallas

Author for correspondence: Curtis Bram, curtis.bram@utdallas.edu

Abstract: Critics of populism and advocates of elitist democracy often place greater confidence in political elites than in the general public. However, this trust may be misplaced. In five experiments with local politicians, state legislators, and members of the public, the author finds a similar willingness across all groups to entrench their party's power when given the opportunity – a self-serving majoritarianism that transcends partisan lines. This tendency is strongest among committed ideologues, politicians running in highly competitive districts, and those who perceive opponents as especially threatening. Local elected officials even appear more focused on securing their party's next presidential victory than on opposing bans against their political rivals. These findings challenge the conventional mass/elite dichotomy, revealing little differences in undemocratic attitudes. Safeguarding democracy likely requires shifting focus from those individual attitudes to strengthening institutional restraints against majority abuses. This title is also available as Open Access on Cambridge Core.

Keywords: American politics, democratic elitism, populism, democratic norms, political elites

ISBNs: 9781009546935 (HB), 9781009546942 (PB), 9781009546898 (OC)
ISSNs: 2633-3368 (online), 2633-335X (print)

Contents

1 "Use My Words against Me"

The sudden death of Justice Antonin Scalia in February 2016 created a vacancy on the Supreme Court, presenting an opportunity for President Obama to nominate a replacement. However, Republican leaders immediately opposed Obama's choice, Merrick Garland, arguing that no nominee should be confirmed until after the November election – more than eight months away – when the public would choose between a Democratic or Republican administration.

"I want you to use my words against me," said Republican Senator Lindsey Graham, claiming that if a Republican president faced a Supreme Court vacancy in an election year, he would advocate waiting until the next term to confirm a justice. Graham claimed his opposition to Obama's nomination was grounded in principle, not partisanship. Yet, in 2020, as that election approached, he reversed this stance, supporting President Trump's conservative nominee without hesitation, less than a month before the 2020 election.

It's not just Lindsey Graham. In 1992, then-Senator Joe Biden argued that the Senate should reject Supreme Court nominations in an election year.[1] One might assume this stance would align Biden with Graham's opposition to Garland in 2016, but instead, Biden backed Obama's nominee. Four years later, Biden denounced Trump's 2020 election-year appointment as "rushed and unprecedented."

Populists often accuse politicians of hypocrisy, pointing to figures like Graham and Biden. Typically, though, politicians' principles are not tested so explicitly, and unambiguous examples of hypocrisy are rare. Graham's and Biden's reversals on election-year appointments stand out not just for their inconsistency, but for providing such straightforward evidence of their willingness to abandon their own prior commitments. While clear examples of explicit hypocrisy are rare, it is possible to systematically examine politicians' commitment to fair political competition through experimental designs. To do this, I ask political leaders to make choices in essentially identical situations, randomly flipping the partisan implications. Typically, it is nearly impossible to observe politicians' underlying motivations or make inferences from their voting behavior. After all, Graham and Biden did not say that their flipping positions were based on partisanship. Instead, both claimed to be relying on democratic principles, and there are reasonable arguments in favor of making (or blocking) Supreme Court appointments just before elections, and both could (and did) claim that their differing stances were based on different situations.

1 Hirschfeld Davis, Julie. "Joe Biden Argued for Delaying Supreme Court Picks in 1992." The New York Times. February 22, 2016.

If nearly identical circumstances had not repeated themselves, observers might never have known that Graham and Biden were not committed to the principle of no election-year Supreme Court appointments.

Despite the difficulty in discovering the true motivations of politicians, a review of decades of research comparing elites and the public concludes that when there are differences, "political elites are clearly more democratic than ordinary publics" (Peffley & Rohrschneider, 2007, 77). Indeed, democratic theory has relied on the idea that "political elites, by virtue of their involvement in politics, outstrip ordinary citizens in commitment to civil liberties and democratic rights" (Sniderman et al., 1996, p. 47). This elitist theory flips the burden of upholding democracy from citizens, who can check the ambitions of power-seeking politicians, to leaders, who will hopefully "restrain the passions of the public" (Sniderman et al., 1996, p. 18). If democratic elitism is true, then politicians are more committed to democratic principles than the citizens they represent.

Today, this older theory of democratic elitism receives little attention, as if the issue has been solved. Instead, contemporary debate often emphasizes the perceived threat posed by populist movements to democratic institutions. One prominent definition describes populism as a worldview that divides society into two homogeneous, opposing groups: "the pure people" and "the corrupt elite" (Mudde, 2004). This populist idea that the people are pure and the elites are corrupt is the exact opposite of what proponents of democratic elitism believe. Mudde even writes that "Elitism is populism's mirror-image: it shares its Manichean worldview, but wants politics to be an expression of the views of the moral elite, instead of the amoral people" (Mudde, 2004, p. 543).

Both democratic elitism and populism share a focus on the divide between elites and the public. While populism views elites as immoral and ready to do anything to hold onto power, elitism considers the public as less capable of understanding democratic principles. This dichotomy raises an empirical question: are politicians more committed to democracy than the people they represent?

If the populists are correct, then the people will be more principled and better able to defend core democratic principles than hypocritical elites. If the elitists are correct, then politicians will restrain the antidemocratic impulses of the people by defending minority political rights. Democracies must struggle with balancing the will of the majority with protections for individual rights. Success depends on institutional constraints and on elected representatives who understand and support this balance, even as individuals differ on the optimum. However, despite the importance of adjudicating between populist and elitist theories, researchers have not experimentally tested the principles of political elites and compared those elites to the public. This is a critical issue. In recent years, a sitting president attempted to remain in office despite losing an election, and many members of Congress voted to help him stay in power. Researchers have explored those cases of elite-driven threats to democratic norms (L. M. Bartels & Carnes, 2023; Jacobson, 2021). But, like the example of Lindsey Graham and Joe Biden earlier, specific examples can only tell us so much about the dichotomy between elites and the masses.

Even as these examples are inherently limited in what they can tell us about the motivations of politicians, researchers are publishing books that seem to lay the blame for today's challenges on the people. Titles include: "The People vs. Democracy" (Mounk, 2018) and "How can populism be defeated?" (Müller, 2018). Thirty years ago, others argued that democracy could endure so long as elites could protect the democratic regime and its norms from the electorate (Sullivan et al., 1993, p. 52). Even before that, some went so far as to write that elites are "substantially less suspicious and cynical than is the electorate" (McClosky, 1964, p. 371).

But my findings indicate that many state- and local-politicians are not more committed to democratic principles than members of the public. This is a new conclusion because contemporary research on democratic principles has focused almost exclusively on mass public opinion. We know from these studies of the American public that the people "cannot be relied on" as a bulwark against populism because "the values undergirding liberal democracy are fragile at the grassroots" (F. E. Lee, 2020, p. 372). This threat of populism is that of majoritarianism with no respect for the minority (Grzymala-Busse, 2017, p. 1). But by conducting experiments with political elites, I show that it is not just populist leaders (or the well-studied mass public) who are willing to dispense with minority political rights. Critics of populism charge populists with illiberal majoritarianism, but I find that the problem is widespread.

These results indicate that many politicians sampled express some willingness to restrict the rights of their political opponents, and their support for antidemocratic policies is not much different from support among public respondents. In some scenarios, respondents were even open to extreme measures, such as policies that would effectively prevent all political opponents from running for statewide office. Overall, these five experiments suggest a dual threat to American democracy – neither citizens nor politicians consistently support fair political competition.

To make the case that populist majoritarianism is more widespread than a handful of leaders' and their supporters, I first follow past research and compare the responses of elites and the masses to descriptive survey responses. When answering abstract survey questions, politicians are more committed to respecting minority political rights than members of the public, and this is consistent with decades of research. But just like the behavior of politicians cannot typically tell us much about their motivations, descriptive data cannot empirically adjudicate between what they say they believe and what they would actually do, especially when faced with realistic and specific scenarios. To differentiate between theories, I instead rely on Sniderman's conceptualization:

> The heart of the theory of democratic elitism, then, comes to this. Although ordinary citizens are supportive of democratic rights in the abstract, they fail to back them when it is necessary to back them in specific political controversies. By contrast, political elites overwhelmingly support democratic rights, even when they are contested. (Sniderman et al., 2000, p. 472)

This points toward a clear test for democratic elitism. When making abstract policy choices about democratic rights, both elites and citizens will uphold democratic principles. But for democratic elitism to hold, when faced with specific policy choices, elites must act to uphold democratic political competition, even as their constituents do not.

All five studies show that when democratic principles explicitly come into conflict with partisan gains, many of today's politicians and members of the public seek to advance their partisan interests. I report results from two types of experiments, each conducted with sitting politicians and members of the public. In these experiments, respondents make choices about policies that either undermine their opponents' chances of winning the next election or curtail their opponents' influence in shaping policy. In total, approximately 300 state legislators and 900 local policymakers participated in these studies, along with about 1,800 members of the public.

The first three experiments rely on a design that varies only whether the respondents' party is in the majority. Some of the most important advances in recent research on support for democratic norms have been the use of new approaches like this to probe the ways that citizens make trade-offs. Researchers find that many Democrats and Republicans want their side to win so badly that they will throw away abstract democratic principles when they believe that doing so comes with partisan benefits (Graham & Svolik, 2020; Simonovits, McCoy, & Littvay, 2022). In these designs, members of the public participate in experiments that ask them to sacrifice some policy or electoral gains to uphold some political principle. I build on these experimental approaches to separate partisan motivations from principled policy support in the minds of politicians.

The fourth and fifth experiments investigate trade-offs in democratic politics, specifically examining the limits of support for policies that restrict minority political rights. Rather than measuring explicit support for antidemocratic policies, I assess politicians' willingness to oppose these policies when doing so incurs a personal or partisan cost. By shifting the analysis from direct support to the opportunity costs of upholding democratic norms, I find that a significant number of politicians and members of the public may be willing to acquiesce to policies with authoritarian implications, especially when partisan gains are at stake. Respondents' opposition to banning all political opponents from statewide office appears weaker than their desire to secure an electoral win. Notably, while local elected leaders seem to prioritize partisan gains over democratic principles, they place even less importance on their own salaries than on preserving fair democratic processes. This suggests that respondents value their side winning more than they value both expressing support for democratic elections and sometimes even their own financial interests.

The findings challenge both populist and elitist assumptions about who can best safeguard democracy, suggesting that neither group alone can be relied upon to ensure democratic stability. As my results suggest that today's politicians are not more committed to democratic principles than the public, critics of populism cannot depend on politicians to protect us from an often antidemocratic public. Many politicians are just like the rest of us, often pursuing partisan advantage with the intent to hold onto power.

Given these findings, I argue for prioritizing institutional safeguards against partisan excesses over trust in the unpredictable attitudes of political elites or the public. Institutional constraints on majority power are as vital today as ever. After the 2024 presidential election, when Republicans led by President Trump regained control of the presidency, House of Representatives, and Senate, Democratic Representative Pramila Jayapal reversed her long-standing support for eliminating the filibuster. This reversal highlights the volatility of elite attitudes toward minority political rights. Jayapal stated plainly: "Am I championing getting rid of the filibuster now, when the [Republicans have] the trifecta? No. But had we had the trifecta, I would have been, because we have to show that government can deliver."[2]

2 Democratic Elitism versus Populism

In 2020, Graham and Svolik asked: when can we expect the public to check the authoritarian impulses of partisan officials? Their findings were stark – partisans often did not withdraw support from leaders engaging in antidemocratic

[2] Freeman, Caitlin. "With Trump set to take power, Jayapal backtracks on ending filibuster." *Seattle Times*.

actions (Graham & Svolik, 2020, p. 394). Yet, public ambivalence toward fundamental principles of political competition is not new (L. M. Bartels et al., 2023, p. 20). Researchers have long found that citizens held divergent views on democracy's core tenets (Prothro & Grigg, 1960). In the 1960s, democratic elitists expected partisan elected officials to resist those authoritarian inclinations among the public.

This expectation appeared reasonable at the time, as survey data consistently showed "regular and substantial" differences in democratic commitment between the public and political leaders (Sullivan et al., 1993, p. 51). In 1964, Herbert McClosky's comparative survey of national convention attendees and the general public revealed a much stronger commitment to democratic norms among elites. As a staunch elitist, McClosky was critical of the "plain, homespun, uninitiated yeoman, worker and farmer," whom he saw as insufficiently dedicated to political institutions (McClosky, 1964, p. 375).

McClosky believed that populist sentiment – the preference for the people over elites, for the "unsophisticated over the sophisticated" – had become conventional wisdom. He viewed his elitist perspective as a necessary counterpoint, attributing populist dominance to a lack of comparative data on public versus elite views. Richard Hofstadter famously described Americans' "populistic dream" of the "omnicompetence of the common man," underscoring the strength of this ideal in American political culture (Hofstadter, 1964, p. 34).

McClosky's elitism directly opposes the central premise of populism, which scholars characterize as a struggle between the people and the elite (Mansbridge & Macedo, 2019; Mudde & Kaltwasser, 2017; Müller, 2017; Thompson, 2017).[3] While McClosky argued that the public's distance from power hindered their understanding of liberal democracy, populists regard elites as inherently immoral – and even undemocratic – precisely because of their proximity to power and distance from the people (Urbinati, 2019, p. 63). For them, proximity to power almost inevitably corrupts politicians (Taggart, 2018, p. 80). This means that for populists, the problem with politicians is often that they have served in government. Serving in elected office goes "hand in hand" with declining moral values (Urbinati, 2019, p. 60). Populists think that little to nothing, and especially not elites, should stand in the way of the people's will.[4]

[3] Some argue that anti-elitism alone is enough to indicate populist attitudes (Rooduijn & Pauwels, 2011, p. 1278).

[4] Populism is a broad concept, and can also include anti-science elements and low efficacy elements (Berman, 2021; Oliver & Rahn, 2016). Furthermore, exclusionary conceptualizations of the people often hang together with populist thinking (Mansbridge & Macedo, 2019).

On the other hand, elitists argue that practical political experience encourages politicians to exercise restraint, prompting a "sober second look" before disrupting democratic norms, even if doing so would align with majority views (Sullivan et al., 1993, p. 53). As Sullivan explains, rather than fostering corruption, government service teaches politicians to consider the reciprocity of political actions – recognizing that any unfair tactic they employ today might be used against them tomorrow. This outlook, though not necessarily principled, reflects an understanding of democracy's delicate balance of power.

Even as elitist and populist perspectives on the effects of serving in government oppose each other (Akkerman, Mudde, & Zaslove, 2014), populists and democratic elitists do not necessarily view elites and the masses through the exact same lens. Populists often contend that politicians are primarily driven by personal gain or enrichment (Mangset et al., 2019), whereas elitists focus on leaders' ostensible commitment to pluralism and democratic principles. Despite these differences, both perspectives revolve around the mass/elites dichotomy, which many theorists consider central to democratic politics (Ober, 1989; Piano, 2019).

Since both populism and elitism center on the relationship between elites and the masses, it is crucial to empirically test the commitments of both groups to liberal democracy. If elites are no less willing to manipulate electoral institutions than the public, this suggests that many politicians are implicit believers in populist majoritarianism, at least when doing so benefits their side. For populists, institutional constraints must not prevent politicians in the majority from enacting the people's will (Riker, 1988, pgs. 11, 249). Indeed, my results indicate that, like populist leaders, many mainstream elected politicians are willing to dispense with restraints on their power when they hold the majority, and with those restraints removed, they may manipulate elections. This is akin to "discriminatory legalism," wherein populists use institutions to treat their own side differently from their opponents (Müller, 2017, p. 46).

While some evidence indicates low support for antidemocratic policies among U.S. state legislators (Druckman, Kang, et al., 2023a), there has been little experimental examination of whether today's politicians would prioritize democratic principles over partisan advantage. The lack of empirical focus on elites is particularly notable given the extensive research into democratic backsliding and antidemocratic attitudes, both internationally (Bermeo, 2016; Eggers, 2014; Gerschewski, 2021; Haggard & Kaufman, 2016; Krishnarajan, 2023; Waldner & Lust, 2018; Wunsch & Gessler, 2023) and within the American public (L. M. Bartels, 2020; Carey et al., 2022; Holliday et al., 2024).

Drawing directly from McClosky and Brill's foundational work, I begin by examining support for liberal-democratic norms in abstract terms. I surveyed local elected officials, such as city councilors and county commissioners, and a sample of the public. My questions probed scenarios where a democratic majority confronts a choice: whether to uphold or suppress minority political rights.[5] Using items directly from McClosky's and Brill's work, enables direct comparison over time (McClosky & Brill, 1983, pgs. 52, 51, and 148). Although these items are from classic elitist research, they clearly resonate with populist majoritarianism (F. E. Lee, 2020, p. 371). The scenarios present a winning majority with the option to respect or override minority rights:

- If the majority votes in a referendum to ban the expression of certain opinions, should the majority opinion be followed?
  - No, because free speech is a more fundamental right than majority rule.
  - Yes, because no group has a greater right than the majority to decide which opinions can or cannot be expressed.
  - Neither / undecided
- When making decisions about public affairs, the majority:
  - Has a duty to respect the rights of the minority.
  - Should be able to do whatever it wants to.
  - Neither / undecided
- Suppose the President and Congress have to violate a constitutional principle to pass an important law the people wanted. Would you support them in this action?
  - No because protecting the constitution is more important to the national welfare than any law could possibly be.
  - Yes, because the Constitution shouldn't be allowed to stand in the way of what the people need and want.
  - Neither / undecided

Figure 1 displays these findings. Descriptively, the results reveal little change since researchers first compared elite and public attitudes toward democratic rights. In the abstract, an overwhelming majority of both politicians and the public endorse minority political rights, even when majority preferences could be enacted. Admittedly, differences in survey mode and sampling strategy caution against strict one-to-one comparisons. Still, if anything has shifted, it appears that today's elites are even more supportive of minority rights than their predecessors. Despite anecdotal evidence suggesting otherwise, these

[5] Other studies have posed McClosky's questions to the mass public, though without including an elite sample (Hicks, McKee, & Smith, 2021).

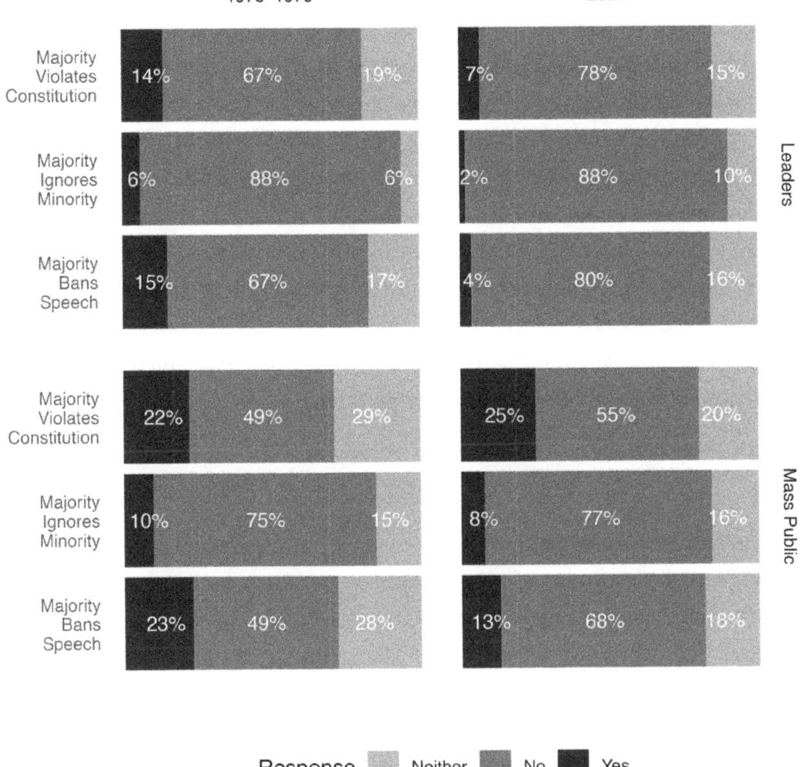

Figure 1 Abstract support for democratic principles. Results from 1978–1979 are taken directly from (McClosky & Brill, 1983, pgs. 52, 51, and 148). McClosky and Brill surveyed attendees to Democrat and Republican national conventions. Results from 2024 come from original surveys of local elected leaders and members of the public.

descriptive data suggest a strong commitment to democracy among contemporary politicians – at least in response to abstract survey questions, where adherence comes at no cost.

The problem is that these questions do not ask politicians or the public to sacrifice anything. They respond to a hypothetical situation where a generic majority disregards the rights of a generic minority. The majority the respondents are considering might even oppose respondents' own interests, incentivizing them to uphold minority rights. To more rigorously test democratic elitism, it is necessary to examine the "heart of the theory," which Sniderman identifies as consistent elite support for democratic principles even when it comes to specific political controversies (Sniderman et al., 2000, p. 472). This suggests that to adjudicate between elitist and populist theories of democracy, it is insufficient to rely on responses to abstract ideals. Instead, it is necessary to probe the motivations of politicians and the public within concrete political scenarios.

This is not just a methodological point. In 1983, Herbert McClosky and Alida Brill observed that politicians are far more likely than the general public to understand which values are reasonable and which are not (McClosky & Brill, 1983, p. 29). This insight highlights a fundamental obstacle in testing democratic elitism: the premise of the theory – heightened political knowledge at the elite level – complicates efforts to assess its validity. If elites grasp what is widely seen as legitimate, then this awareness exacerbates social desirability bias in surveys. Such bias not only undermines the validity of descriptive survey data on politicians' motivations but also complicates interpretations of their rhetoric. To circumvent social desirability bias, I use experiments to explore what motivates politicians' support for policies.[6]

2.1 Why Politicians Support Policies

Understanding politicians' motives is essential to adjudicating between populist and elitist expectations for politicians' behavior, as both theories hinge on the principles guiding elites. While both elitists and populists view the divide between politicians and the public as fundamentally moral, their predictions are oppositional: elitists believe that elites are superior, while populists hold that the public is more virtuous. The central issue lies in these theories' shared claim about the underlying motivations of politicians versus the people. Both offer clear predictions, but testing those predictions is difficult. Populists can always point to elite hypocrisy, while elitists cite troubling survey results from the public. Each side can attribute the other's actions to partisan interests or hypocrisy, reinforcing their respective narratives.

However, motivations are difficult to infer from behavior alone. Take, for instance, North Carolina's Republican-backed 2013 voter-identification law. The vote split sharply along partisan lines: seventy-three Republicans supported it, while forty-one Democrats opposed it.[7] At first glance, this could appear to be a partisan power play – both parties acting on the belief that voter ID laws influence turnout among Democratic-leaning groups. Republicans might support the law as a means to secure advantage, and Democrats might oppose it solely to maintain their base's access to the ballot.

[6] Even before researchers turned their attention to the possibility of democratic backsliding in America, there had been little experimental research on political elites (Peffley & Rohrschneider, 2007, p. 77).

[7] NC General Assembly House Roll Call Vote Transcript for Roll Call # 1337, 2013–2014 Session

Yet this interpretation is only one of many possibilities. Politicians can cite a wide range of justifications for supporting voter ID laws. They might have sincere concerns over illegal voting, worry about foreign interference from adversaries like Russia or China, or simply believe in incentivizing ID ownership without making it mandatory. Opponents may also have varied reasons for not wanting to enact voter ID laws – ranging from ensuring ballot access and preventing undue burdens on disadvantaged groups to pointing out low rates of voter fraud and the costs associated with changing electoral rules.

The partisan divide on this vote does not even confirm that politicians are simply motivated by partisanship. Policy preferences often align with partisan identity (Fowler, 2020). Republicans may all sincerely believe that voter ID laws serve the public good, and their identification with the Republican Party could stem, in part, from this belief. Research indicates that Republican support for voter ID laws persists even when experimental treatments show that such laws might increase minority turnout (Clayton, 2023). If support were purely about suppressing opposition turnout, learning that voter ID laws boost minority turnout should reduce Republican support, yet it does not.

In the specific case of North Carolina's 2013 voter ID bill, we have little to no evidence regarding the motivations of the 114 legislators who voted on it. They may have been driven by sincere beliefs in the policy's merits or by hope for securing partisan advantages. Motivations are what differentiate principled views from cynical power grabs, yet all we can observe are behaviors. However, one Republican official, Precinct Chairman Don Yelton, openly stated that the law would "kick the Democrats in the Butt."[8] Though Yelton's colleagues distanced themselves from his comment and he later resigned, we cannot know that his colleagues' were sincere. He was probably not alone in his view, and his remark serves as a rare, candid example. Still, even here Yelton's stance could still result from a genuine belief that Democrats engage in high levels of illegal voting.

In sum, perfect partisan divides in voting can support a variety of narratives about underlying motivations, but partisan divides do not provide evidence that all members of one party are principled defenders of democracy or that all members of another party are unprincipled partisans. Because observed behavior typically cannot distinguish genuine support from partisan motivation, researchers often rely on survey data to better understand elite behavior (Peffley & Rohrschneider, 2007, 77). However, survey data also present challenges in assessing elite principles.

[8] Blake, Aaron, "Republicans keep admitting that voter ID helps them win, for some reason." *The Washington Post*, April 7, 2016.

Politicians, more so than the public, may be aware of the "right" answers, making elite surveys particularly susceptible to social desirability bias. Returning to the example of Supreme Court confirmations, a politician's response to an abstract question about election-year nominations may not reflect how they would act when presented with an opportunity to secure an ideologically aligned seat on the Supreme Court, potentially for decades.

People tend to rationalize support for antidemocratic policies that align with partisan interests (Krishnarajan, 2023). Politicians may support the principles underlying policies that benefit their side, while simultaneously disavowing similar policies if the advantage is uncertain or works against them.[9] In this work, the first three experiments tackle the issue of political motivations by attempting to separate principled support from self-serving partisanship.

2.2 What Counts as Antidemocratic

The checks on majority power that I explore in the first set of experiments safeguard minority political rights (Elster, 1994; Zürn, 2022). These anti-majoritarian limits on what a winning faction can do align with a long tradition of American political thought. The Founders were deeply concerned about the dangers of empowered majorities (Madison, 1787). John Adams extended this concern to skepticism about partisan divisions,[10] while Thomas Jefferson went further, famously saying, "If I could not go to heaven but with a party, I would not go there at all."[11]

But a second challenge beyond discerning elite motivations is the inherent ambiguity of what counts as democratic. Elitist and populist theories hold fundamentally opposing views on the majority's role: populists believe that little should obstruct the majority's will (F. E. Lee, 2020, p. 371), whereas elitists expect politicians to protect minority rights by demonstrating "extraordinary forbearance and self-discipline" to "place constraints upon the use of our collective power" (McClosky, 1964, p. 376).

The balance between majority control and minority rights has been a central question since Plato. The framers of the American Constitution prioritized minority rights, aware of the potential impact of partisanship on democratic elections. Yet, the American system is not the only democratic model. Another approach is pure majoritarianism. Although such a populist democracy risks

[9] This aligns with earlier work showing that Democrats and Republicans often view policies from their own party as more effective simply because they originate from co-partisans (Druckman, Peterson, & Slothuus, 2013, p. 59). See also: (Druckman & Bolsen, 2011).

[10] From John Adams to Jonathan Jackson, 2 October 1780. National Archives.

[11] From Thomas Jefferson to Francis Hopkinson, 13 March 1789. National Archives.

infringing on individual rights – a core principle of liberal democracy – it remains democratic (Galston, 2017, p. 3). Empirical evidence even suggests that many people view majority decisions as inherently democratic (Grossman et al., 2022).

Reasonable people can disagree on just about everything in politics. Populists, for example, may argue that confirming a Supreme Court nominee just before an election undermines voters' right to be heard, particularly if public dissatisfaction with the current administration is high. Others might counter that an elected president has the authority to make appointments until the day their term ends. This fundamental contestability of democratic values poses a challenge for empirical research on antidemocratic attitudes, as reasonable disagreements certainly extend to issues like voter ID laws, gerrymandering, and the judiciary's role in democracy (Sniderman et al., 1996).

But this contestation does not extend to a potential ban on all opponents from running for all offices statewide. The second set of experiments present respondents with this blatantly authoritarian option. Such a move does not align with any democratic principle, as it would deny voters any opportunity to make their voices heard. Democratic elitism predicts that politicians would remain "firmly anchored to an ongoing commitment to democratic principles and institutions" (Peffley & Rohrschneider, 2007, p. 66). If politicians are committed to this high standard, they would reject such a policy outright, even when doing so accompanies other difficult choices.

By contrast, when populist politicians gain power, they often undermine checks and balances, "manipulat[ing] electoral institutions to cement their power against challenge" (F. E. Lee, 2020, p. 371).[12] Populists justify these actions by claiming that their party defends the "real" people against opposition parties, whom they portray as representing harmful cultural outsiders (Vachudova, 2021, p. 472). This outlook suggests that populists will disregard liberal-democratic constraints, believing they represent a "silent majority" regardless of actual support (Mudde, 2004; Urbinati, 2019).[13]

My analysis focuses on populist majoritarianism and the potential for partisan politics to restrict minority rights. The findings show that it is not only populists but also mainstream politicians who are open to manipulating political institutions. Politicians from both major parties, Democrats and Republicans alike, demonstrate a willingness to consider using majority power

[12] Lee's claim draws on extensive comparative research on populism (Hawkins & Littvay, 2019; Houle & Kenny, 2018; Huber & Schimpf, 2016; Kenny, 2017; Ruth, 2018).

[13] Some see this ambiguity in who counts as a member of the demos or community as a key feature of populism (Howarth, 2014, p. 127). Others have argued that populism is not very helpful in targeting subgroups of people (Mudde & Kaltwasser, 2017, p. 47).

in scenarios where it will disadvantage their political opponents. This suggests that neither elitists nor populists are correct in viewing one side of the elite-mass dichotomy as more moral by virtue of the commitment to fair political competition.

2.3 Who Counts as an Elite

In selecting elite participants for these experiments, I concentrated on elected officials, departing from McClosky's original approach. McClosky broadly defined elites as those who shape public opinion or exhibit greater political knowledge and engagement (McClosky & Zaller, 1984, 13). That inclusive operationalization aligns with recent studies, such as surveys examining elite/mass divides through party activists, social media influencers, and campaigners (Layman, Lee, & Wolbrecht, 2023). By focusing specifically on elected politicians, my study narrows this definition, isolating elites with formal political authority. In an era where partisan and independent media dilute the influence of nonelected opinion leaders (Bram, 2024), holding greater political knowledge alone likely no longer suffices as a marker of elite status. Focusing on elected officials does shrink the scope of the elite for these studies, and it is possible that as candidate quality has fallen and officeholders have become more extreme (Hall, 2019), this focus on politicians underestimates the commitment of nonelected elites to democratic norms. Still, the politicians participating in these experiments make real decisions about American electoral institutions and the scope of majority power, at a time when those decisions will determine the future of American democracy.

To recruit elected politicians to participate in these studies, I first worked with CivicPulse, a nonprofit organization that maintains records of American government officials, on two separate studies of local elected leaders. Results from CivicPulse surveys are widely reported in academic studies (N. Lee et al., 2022; Mullin & Hansen, 2023; Shaffer et al., 2020). These two samples were designed (by random draw from a comprehensive list of all local elected leaders) to be representative of top elected officials and governing board members serving in U.S. township, municipality, and county governments for communities with populations of 1,000 or more. These two studies involved 988 officials. Second, I directly emailed all state legislators with a publicly available email address. That study of state legislators recruited 308 respondents. Finally, I recruited two online, opt-in general population samples for comparing treatment effects in the elite surveys to the public. Table 1 shows the study populations, recruitment sources, and sample sizes.

Table 1 Study populations, recruitment sources, and sample sizes.

Study Population	Recruitment Source	Sample Size
Local Elected Officials (Study 1)	CivicPulse	486
State Legislators (Study 2)	Direct Email	308
General Public (Study 3)	Lucid	1,012
Local Elected Officials (Study 4)	CivicPulse	502
General Public (Study 5)	CloudResearch	1,004

3 Elites Are Not More Principled than the Public

I employed two experimental approaches to probe the motivations driving political leaders and the public, confronting the two challenges I have outlined: the difficulty of discerning motivations solely from behavior, and the ambiguities surrounding what qualifies as democratic behavior. According to elitist critics of populism, elected officials display a stronger commitment to democratic principles than the public. My first type of experiment (on restricting minority political rights and manipulating elections) probes politicians' commitment to these principles through scenarios that closely reflect their real-world responsibilities. This design engages elected leaders with policies directly relevant to the daily operations of state and local governance, such as gerrymandering and judicial manipulation.

Recent scholarship has found that partisans often prioritize political gain over adherence to democratic principles (B. L. Bartels & Johnston, 2020; Graham & Svolik, 2020; Simonovits et al., 2022). Those studies usually involve public participants, who are asked to forgo some policy or electoral advantage to preserve a liberal-democratic principle. Building on this work, this first experimental design examines how politicians respond in scenarios where the majority holds the power to curtail minority rights. The treatment and control conditions vary only in whether the respondent's own party is in the majority, isolating whether elites support minority rights only when they may be in the minority themselves. This exposes potential hypocrisy, revealing whether elites champion minority protections under threat of losing power but favor majoritarianism when assured of their own dominance.

To distinguish partisan self-interest from genuine support for minority rights among politicians, this first experimental design builds on the concept of a "partisan veil-of-ignorance" (Flanders, 2012). In the control condition, respondents have no knowledge of whether a policy shift will work to their party's advantage or detriment. This probes politicians' respect for minority rights by testing their commitment to fair political competition. Political theory suggests that under uncertainty, decision-makers will choose systems that ensure favorable outcomes if they end up in the least powerful minority position (McGann, 2006, p. 100). Applied to electoral politics, this implies that partisan politicians, when they have no idea whether Republicans or Democrats stand to benefit, would support fair and balanced rules.

Because respondents in the control group do not know whether the proposed policy will benefit their party, the aim is for them to use impartial reasoning (Frohlich & Oppenheimer, 1992, p. 15).[14] This should allow for a more pure assessment of politicians' stance on electoral rules. By keeping all other variables constant between experimental conditions, the differential support between scenarios separates belief in the merits of a policy from the influence of partisanship. If politicians only endorse measures that curtail the competitiveness of minorities when it serves their partisan aims, then they prioritize their political goals over principled policy support.

Recent work finds that politicians exhibit notably lower antidemocratic tendencies than the general public and maintain relatively accurate perceptions of their partisan base (Druckman, Kang, et al., 2023a, p. 2). Yet, I anticipate that both politicians and the public will show a heightened tendency to endorse antidemocratic policies when their partisan interests are at stake. To test this, the first hypothesis (H1) examines the level of politicians' support for these policies. Specifically, I analyze the impact of treatment assignment, which manipulates information regarding which party controls a hypothetical government, on respondents' levels of policy endorsement.[15]

The second hypothesis (H2) centers on respondents' perceptions of their in-party colleagues and out-party opponents, particularly under scenarios where these groups hold legislative control. This hypothesis is useful for evaluating elitist versus populist theories, as each anticipates different outcomes. If elitists are correct in asserting that government service has a moderating influence, politicians may expect equitable treatment from their political rivals.

This analysis of politicians' perceptions of their peers extends recent research that links "meta-perceptions" – beliefs about the political attitudes and actions of others – to the prevailing climate of political polarization (Braley et al., 2023; Lees & Cikara, 2020; Moore-Berg et al., 2020). Research shows that individuals with extreme political views often assume others hold similarly intense positions (Westfall et al., 2015). These distorted perceptions

[14] See also: (Frohlich, Oppenheimer, & Eavey, 1987).

[15] The dependent variable is the cumulative level of policy support, measured on a seven-point scale.

may stem from an overemphasis on political conflict (Bram, 2023b) and are particularly relevant for understanding antidemocratic attitudes. Indeed, support for such policies may be driven by pessimistic assumptions about others' intentions (Mernyk et al., 2022).

I preregistered these two hypotheses for the local policymaker and general population surveys, and in all three studies, I found strong evidence for both.[16]

- H1: Respondents will support antidemocratic policies at higher rates when those policies benefit their own political side.
- H2: Respondents will overestimate the extent of support for antidemocratic policies among their political opponents.

To test these hypotheses, all respondents engaged in experiments featuring policy scenarios where members of a hypothetical state legislature or local government (distinct from their own) proposed policy changes aimed at limiting the power of the minority party. In the treatment group, respondents were asked to support or oppose policies that would specifically favor their own party, as the scenario established that their party controlled both the legislature and executive roles (or the governing board). Conversely, respondents in the control group evaluated these policies without knowing which party would gain a policy or electoral advantage. The scenarios in the state legislator study were adapted from Voelkel et al. (2023), who examined similar policies in their exploration of affective polarization's impact on antidemocratic attitudes among the public. For the survey of local policymakers, scenarios were tailored to address relevant local issues and specified control by the governing board and the top executive position, typically the mayor.

In practical terms, this design focuses on a specific type of democratic transgression: power-consolidating changes to democratic institutions (Ahmed, 2023, p. 968). The policies examined are those that restrict the ability of minority parties to compete or shape policy. Such policy changes are arguably among the most hazardous for democratic integrity (Scheppele, 2018). For each group of politicians, I present two policy scenarios. One scenario addresses electoral fairness, echoing a broader concern in recent work on democratic backsliding within U.S. states (J. Grumbach, 2022, p. 163). The second scenario centers on diminishing the minority party's influence. By comparing politicians' choices in scenarios where they are aware or unaware of their own party's potential advantage, the experiments reveal whether these leaders are likely to uphold respect for political opponents if they hold majority power in reality. Table 2

[16] The preregistration is available at: https://osf.io/az4vb. Data and code to replicate the analysis for all five studies are available at: https://doi.org/10.7910/DVN/HHYVG6.

Table 2 Survey scenarios for assessing principled policy support.

Policy Scenarios

Scenarios for State Legislators

Gerrymandering

Imagine that **(Pipe in in-party / legislators if in control group) in control of a state legislature** have drafted a proposal that would **allow the governor (a Pipe in in-party / delete if control)** to appoint **all** members of the committee which draws voting district lines.

A bipartisan committee of state legislators currently draws voting district lines.

Judicial Appointments

Imagine that **(Pipe in in-party / legislators if control) in control of a state legislature** have drafted a proposal to nominate and vote on judges in groups.

This would make it more difficult for *(pipe in out-party / the party in the minority if control)* to object to the appointment of judges.

Scenarios for Local Policymakers

Making One Party More Likely to Win Elections

Imagine that **(Pipe in in-party / officials if control) in control of a local government** have drafted a proposal to switch the election of governing board members from district voting to at-large voting.

The proposal would help make [Pipe in in-party's who / members of the party that] currently controls the board, more likely to win their races.

Stacking Board Membership

Imagine that **(Pipe in in-party / officials if control) in control of a local government** are considering a proposal to increase the size of the governing board.

The proposal will allow the top official (a [pipe in in-party / delete if control]) to appoint new members, who will serve until their seats can be voted upon in the next election.

outlines the policy scenarios presented to both local policymakers and state legislators.

There is variation between the policy issues shown in Table 2, with some (gerrymandering) seeming to more closely reflect the status quo than others (increasing the size of the city council by adding copartisans). This might suggest that support for at least some of these policy issues cannot really be antidemocratic, since one could think that they reflect the reality of current politics (Ahmed, 2023, p. 970). However, I explicitly designed these scenarios so that all four reflect a meaningful departure from the status quo. In the gerrymandering scenario, respondents are told that it is a bipartisan committee that currently draws district lines and that the replacement will be completely partisan. While this realism enriches the findings, it also introduces interpretive challenges: the policies politicians support or oppose inevitably blur the boundaries between democratic and undemocratic actions. The inherent ambiguity in what is or is not democratic naturally leads to the second experimental design, introduced in Section 5, that incorporates unambiguously antidemocratic policies.

3.1 Study 1: Local Elected Officials

These sections present findings from three studies that examine principled policy support. I begin with results from the sample of local elected officials, followed by data from a study of current state legislators, and conclude with insights from a general population sample.[17]

The first study was conducted as part of a nationwide online survey involving 486 local government officials, organized by CivicPulse between May 10, 2023, and June 27, 2023. This study included representatives from townships (130), municipalities (290), and counties (66). CivicPulse validates their contact list by contracting with a company that reaches out to every local government in the sample frame every three months. This ensures that the invitation links are sent to the specific official randomly selected for survey participation, and not to a generic government email. Respondents received no financial incentives to complete the survey, reducing the likelihood of participation by non-intended recipients. According to CivicPulse, 7.3% of those invited to participate began the survey, with 3.7% completing it and thus being included in the dataset I received. Table 3 provides a comparison between the survey sample and the sample frame. Median values were calculated from ungrouped data across three geographic categories in the respondent metadata. Of these respondents, 432 were partisans who completed the experiment and are used for the analysis. In this group, 55% were Republicans and 45% were Democrats. Table 4 shows summary demographic statistics for the sample of local policymakers.

Because local policymakers focus on local issues, I designed policy scenarios to measure respondents' willingness to weaken the influence of political

[17] These three studies received approval from Duke University's Institutional Review Board (protocol # 2023–0305).

Table 3 Comparison of survey sample with full population medians.

	Population Size	College Educated	Democratic Vote Share
Sample Frame	4,954	21%	39%
Sample	5,804	27%	46%

Table 4 Demographic characteristics of partisan local policymakers.

Variable	Summary Statistics (SD)
Mean Age	62.02 (12.08)
Mean Education	5.44 (1.47)
Proportion Non-White	0.11
Proportion Female	0.32
Proportion Democrat	0.45
Proportion Republican	0.55
Total Respondents	432

minorities in their jurisdictions. In the first scenario, respondents considered a proposal to shift governing board elections from district-based voting to at-large voting.[18] In this scenario, respondents were explicitly informed that the proposed change would increase the likelihood of the incumbent party retaining control (with the incumbent party varying by experimental condition). In the second scenario, local policymakers were asked to consider a proposal to expand the governing board by allowing the top official (specified as a Democrat for Democrat respondents, Republican for Republican respondents, or left unspecified in the control condition) to appoint additional members, effectively diminishing the minority's ability to influence policy.

Consistent with the preregistered hypotheses, these local policymakers are much more likely (by approximately 17 percentage points, $p < 0.0001$) to support policies that weaken minority political rights when their party would definitely benefit (Figure 2). Responses were coded on a scale from 0 to 1, where 0 equals "Strongly oppose," 0.5 is an equivocal "Neither support nor oppose," and 1 means that a respondent "Strongly support[s]" the policy.[19]

[18] District (or ward-based) voting equates to single-member districts, while at-large voting involves all residents voting for all governing board members (Todd, Bram, & Krishnamurthy, 2024).

[19] Due to the way the study was administered, all local policymakers were either in the treatment or control for both policy scenarios. Because of this, I use a simple model that averages

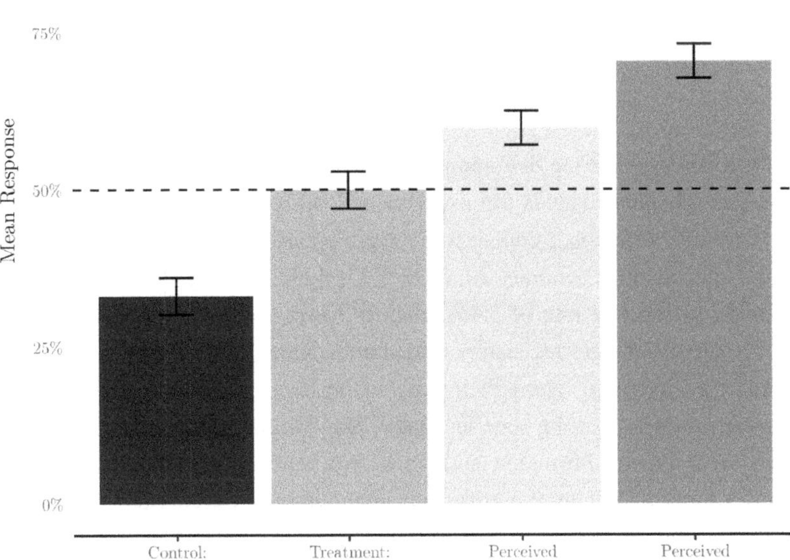

Figure 2 Support for policies when the party that would benefit is unspecified (Control) and when policymakers' own party would benefit (Treatment). This figure also includes policymakers' beliefs about the level of support these policies would receive from their own side and from their opponents.

I also asked all respondents how they thought Democrats and Republicans in their local governing board would act if in the majority (so the policies would benefit the party of the group respondents are reporting their beliefs about). I again coded all responses to range from 0 to 1, where 0 represents no expected support among the members of one of the two parties, and 1 represents 100% support. I asked questions on this scale and coded the responses in this way to facilitate comparability between these types of questions. The third and fourth columns of Figure 2 include the results. These politicians are much more likely to believe that their own colleagues and opponents will support such policies. The respondents believed that 60% of their copartisan policymakers would vote

responses to both scenarios. See the Online Appendix (Section 4) for more information on how this differs from the state legislator survey where I independently randomized treatment assignment.

for policies that restrict the power of those in the minority and that 70% of their opponents would do the same.

The Online Appendix (Section 4.2) includes additional data on treatment effects disaggregated by policy scenario, controls for partisanship, a repeat of the analysis with CivicPulse-supplied weights, and finally demographic factors that may affect attitudes toward democratic institutions, such as education (Cheruvu, 2023).

3.2 Study 2 : State Legislators

With polarization on the rise among state legislatures (Shor & McCarty, 2022), this second study extends the experimental design from local policymakers to state-level officials. I contacted all state legislators with publicly available email addresses on February 20, 2023.[20] Of these, 308 legislators responded, yielding a response rate of 5.4%, slightly lower than the response rate in a recent survey of state legislators (Druckman, Kang, et al., 2023a).[21] Respondents were asked to report their state of residence, partisan affiliation, and current status as a sitting state legislator. Non-sitting legislators and independents were excluded from the analysis, as independents are not relevant to this study's focus on potential partisan advantage in policy scenarios. The sample used for analysis consists of 55% Democrats and 45% Republicans.

Since all state legislators with available email addresses were contacted, this survey constitutes a probability sample for the population of state legislators with public emails. Unlike opt-in online panel studies, this design enables assessment of the sample's representativeness. On average, respondents make up about 5% of each state's legislative seats, with a median representation of approximately 4%.

The coverage rate varies significantly across states, with a standard deviation of approximately 3% (see Table 5). New Hampshire is particularly well-represented, with the sample capturing 15% of its legislature. Given New Hampshire's unusually large legislative body, this elevated response rate could reflect legislators discussing the survey among themselves. At the other extreme, Oklahoma's representation in the sample is only 0.7%, highlighting a need for caution when generalizing results across states. Of course California, with no public contact information, has 0% representation in this experiment. Nonetheless, studies indicate that probability samples like this one generally

---

[20] A total of 5,719 email addresses were sourced from OpenStates.org on February 7, 2023.

[21] Detailed information on sample composition is available in the Online Appendix (Section 5.2).

Table 5 Three most represented, three legislatures with about average representation, and three least represented state legislatures in this sample. The percentage of seats is calculated by taking the number of respondents to the survey and dividing it by the number of seats in the legislature. These numbers for each legislature may vary due to redistricting or other changes.

State		# Respondents	Legislative Seats	% of Seats
Top 3	NH	62	424	14.6%
	NC	20	170	11.8%
	Utah	10	104	9.6%
Middle 3	Iowa	7	150	4.7%
	Nebraska	2	49	4.1%
	Wisconsin	5	132	3.8%
Bottom 3	Arkansas	1	135	0.7%
	Michigan	1	148	0.7%
	Oklahoma	1	149	0.7%
			Mean for All States	4.6%

provide more accurate results than convenience samples, even when response rates are lower (MacInnis et al., 2018).[22]

In the first scenario, respondents were asked whether they would support a proposal to replace a bipartisan committee of legislators responsible for drawing voting districts with one appointed entirely by the partisan governor. In the second scenario, legislators were asked about their willingness to support a proposal to discontinue individual confirmation votes for judges in favor of group confirmations, which would reduce the minority party's influence over judicial appointments. These policies were selected because they both align with the willingness to endorse measures that diminish the power of the minority party.

The first two columns of Figure 3 display the control and treatment effects. Responses were again coded on the same scale from 0 to 1, where 0 indicates "Strongly oppose," 0.5 represents "Neither support nor oppose," and 1 signifies "Strongly support." In the control group, the average support level is 0.34, while in the treatment group, support rises to 0.46. This indicates that legislators are approximately 12 percentage points more likely to endorse policies that advantage their own party compared to identical policies presented

[22] Some researchers argue that online probability samples strike an optimal balance between sample quality and self-report accuracy (Chang & Krosnick, 2009).

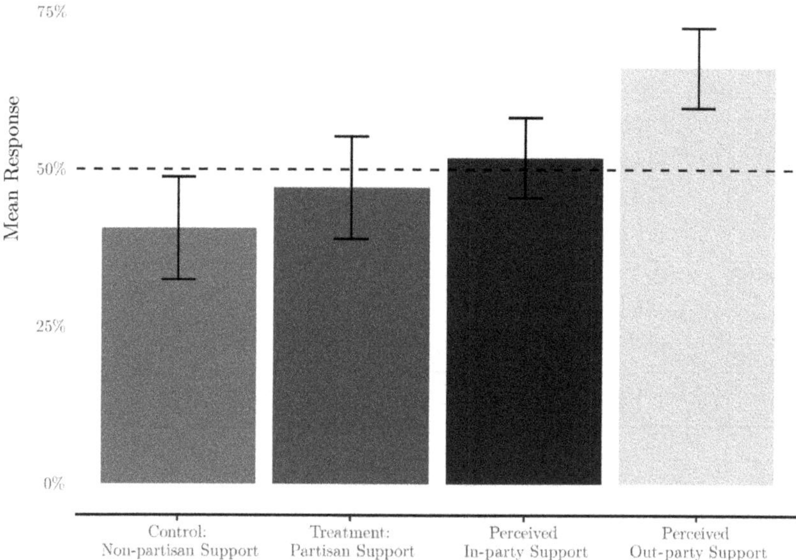

Figure 3 Support for policies when the party that would benefit is unspecified (Control) and when state legislators' own party would benefit (Treatment). This figure also includes legislators' beliefs about the level of support these policies would receive from their own side and from their opponents.

in an abstract context ($p < 0.0001$). Substantively, this result suggests that the average respondent in the control condition opposes these measures, yet becomes more likely to support them when they offer a political advantage. Treatment assignments were randomized independently across scenarios to maximize sample efficiency, with standard errors clustered at the respondent level and a control variable included for the specific scenario under consideration. The findings remain generally consistent when each scenario is analyzed separately (see the Online Appendix Section 5.3).

Just like with the local policymakers, I also found that state legislators believe that their own party would be more supportive of the policy than they, in fact, are, with an average expectation that just over half of the legislators from their party would support the policy. In particular, legislators believe that

70% of their political opponents in their legislature would support policies that restrict minority rights.

3.3 Study 3: General Public

The results from these surveys of politicians can be compared to those from a general population survey, which is crucial for evaluating elitist versus populist theories of democracy. Previous research indicates that many citizens are inclined to support antidemocratic policies that favor their side (Graham & Svolik, 2020; Simonovits et al., 2022), yet other recent studies show widespread opposition to such policies within the American public (Holliday et al., 2024).

To establish a comparison group, I used Lucid, an online opt-in panel provider, to recruit 1,012 participants. Although these nonprobability samples present many potential biases (Jerit & Barabas, 2023), my primary focus is on measuring experimental treatment effects rather than deriving point estimates (Mullinix et al., 2015).[23] The goal here is to compare the experimental treatment effects observed among the public to those found among politicians. The survey included 829 partisans, and they were presented with the same questions posed to state legislators and local government officials. Respondents completed all four independently randomized policy scenarios, identical to those given to the state and local officials. Since neither the state legislator nor local policymaker scenarios directly correspond to the experiences of the general public, there was no compelling reason to limit the public survey to only one set of scenarios. Randomizing across these four scenarios also increased the effective sample size for analysis.

In the control condition, where respondents cannot anticipate which party would benefit, the average level of support for antidemocratic policies is 0.44. In the treatment condition, where respondents know their party will benefit, support rises to 0.56 on the 0-to-1 scale. This 11 percentage-point effect is similar to what I observed among state legislators but slightly smaller than the effect found with local policymakers. Unlike the politician surveys, members of the public are nearly as pessimistic about their own side as they are about their political opponents. Respondents estimate that 62% of their copartisans would support policies favoring their side, compared to 64% support from their opponents – a minor but statistically significant difference. Figure 4 shows these results.

[23] Respondents did not complete the survey and were not included in the dataset if they failed to pass either of two pre-treatment attention checks. See the Online Appendix (Section 6.2) for more.

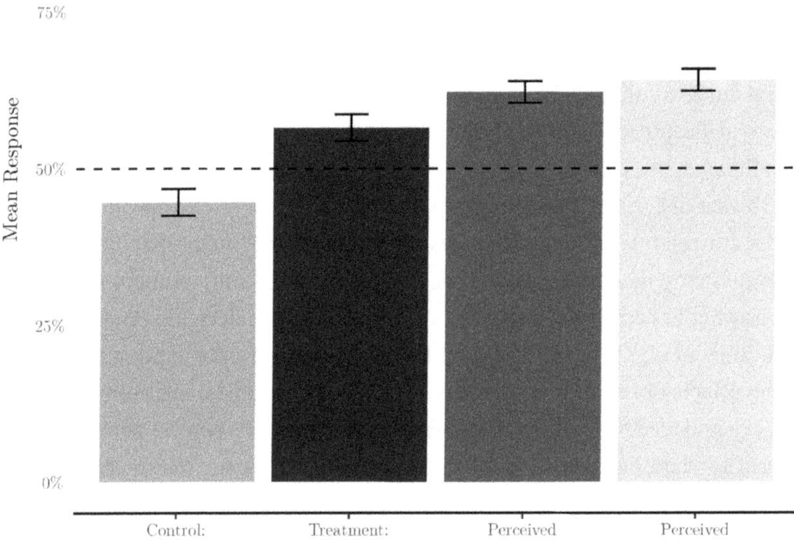

Figure 4 Support for policies when the party that would benefit is unspecified (Control) and when public respondents' own party would benefit (Treatment). This figure also includes general population beliefs about the level of support these policies would receive from politicians on their own side and from their opponents.

4 How Ideology, Electoral Competition, and Perceived Threat Undermine Politicians' Principles

The increased support for policies that restrict minority political rights, when respondents are aware of partisan advantages or disadvantages, suggests that politicians may not be more principled in their policy choices than the public. Although the average treatment effects offer insights into the extent of principled decision-making among sitting politicians, they do not account for the underlying mechanisms driving unprincipled support for antidemocratic policies. Populists and elitists alike might expect meaningful differences between political elites and the public, particularly regarding principled behavior. Several mechanisms could drive such differences, including politicians' ideological commitments, the pressures of reelection, and concerns about their opponents being even worse. This section empirically tests how each of these concerns drive political behavior.

To explore these potential mechanisms, the first CivicPulse-run survey of local policymakers gathered additional data on officials' ideology and the level of partisan competition in their county. Testing these mechanisms with a sample of local politicians is a conservative approach, as local politics is not always partisan or ideological and often depends on the types of issues that local governments address (Anzia, 2021, p. 136). Specifically, local elected leaders might feel that they benefit less from filling their governments with copartisans and may find it easier to work with colleagues across the aisle. If true, then this would likely reduce the magnitude of any interaction between ideological intensity, political competition, and treatment effects in the experiment.[24]

4.1 Politicians Are Ideologues

In 1960, McClosky observed that those who enter politics differ markedly from those who do not. Politics, he argued, "makes great demands on the time, money, and energies of its practitioners – sacrifices that they can more easily justify if they believe they are serving worthwhile social goals" (McClosky, Hoffmann, & O'Hara, 1960, p. 421). This implies that ideologues, or "true believers," are more likely to enter politics. Elitists contend that people willing to enter politics are systematically different from those who are not, with these differences pointing toward more democratic attitudes linked to civic-mindedness (Schubert, Dye, & Zeigler, 2015).

Today, those entering politics remain systematically unrepresentative of their constituents, often having more wealth (Carnes, 2013; Gulzar, 2021), but many are now also deeply committed liberals and conservatives. Political parties have sorted ideologically, with liberals running as Democrats and conservatives as Republicans (Levendusky, 2009). Consequently, there are now fewer moderate Republicans or Democrats serving in office (Amlani & Algara, 2021).

At the candidate entry stage, ideologically polarized candidates now dominate (Fiorina, 2017; Thomsen, 2014).[25] This may be because service in high-level government has become less appealing for centrists, as they must work and argue with strong ideologues from both sides (Thomsen, 2017). Even when moderate candidates are open to collaboration, the benefits of a political

[24] Using this sample instead of the state legislator study was necessary because that survey was designed to be brief to maximize the response rate and did not include additional questions beyond basic demographics and experimental scenarios.

[25] Formal models of candidate entry also emphasize the ideology of incumbents and challengers (Besley & Coate, 1997; Osborne & Slivinski, 1996).

career have declined relative to other professions (Hall, 2019). As a result, those who enter politics tend to be more ideologically extreme, with only those deeply committed to their views willing to accept the trade-offs involved in political service.

When centrists no longer run, their more ideologically driven replacements may prioritize securing and retaining power, potentially because intense ideologues think that their opponents would do terrible things. Rising polarization in Congress is associated with "obstruction, conflict, partisan unity, and narrower majorities" (Algara & Johnston, 2022). To examine the effect of ideological fervor among politicians, I interact policymakers' reported ideology with treatment assignment.

Respondents are coded as having a moderate or weak ideology if they identify as moderate, somewhat liberal, or somewhat conservative. This group comprises 76% of the sample. Strong ideologues, the remaining 24%, identify as very conservative or very liberal. I find that those strong ideologues appear less inclined to support these policy scenarios in the control condition but show about 15 percentage points increased support under the treatment condition where they have the potential to secure partisan advantage. All respondents in this analysis are partisans, so the comparison here is between more moderate Democrats with strongly liberal Democrats, and more moderate Republicans with strongly conservative Republicans. Figure 5 shows this interaction.

This result aligns with related findings among the public that moderates are more likely to uphold democratic principles (Graham & Svolik, 2020, p. 393). Likewise, I found that strong liberal and conservative politicians are far more likely to support antidemocratic policies than their more moderate counterparts in both parties.

4.2 Elections Are Competitive

In addition to the increasing ideological intensity among today's politicians, political elites now face greater instability in political control, accompanied by heightened competition for majority status. As Fiorina observed, between 1954 and 1992, nineteen national elections produced only three patterns of institutional control, whereas since 1992, twelve elections have yielded six different patterns (Fiorina, 2017, p. 4).

Ongoing competition directs politicians' focus toward the "quest for partisan advantage" (F. E. Lee, 2016, p. 160). This shift incentivizes politicians to support antidemocratic policies. Where the responsibility of governance once prompted caution, today's unstable majorities and pressures to retain seats drive politicians to act swiftly on policy initiatives or secure their hold on power – it

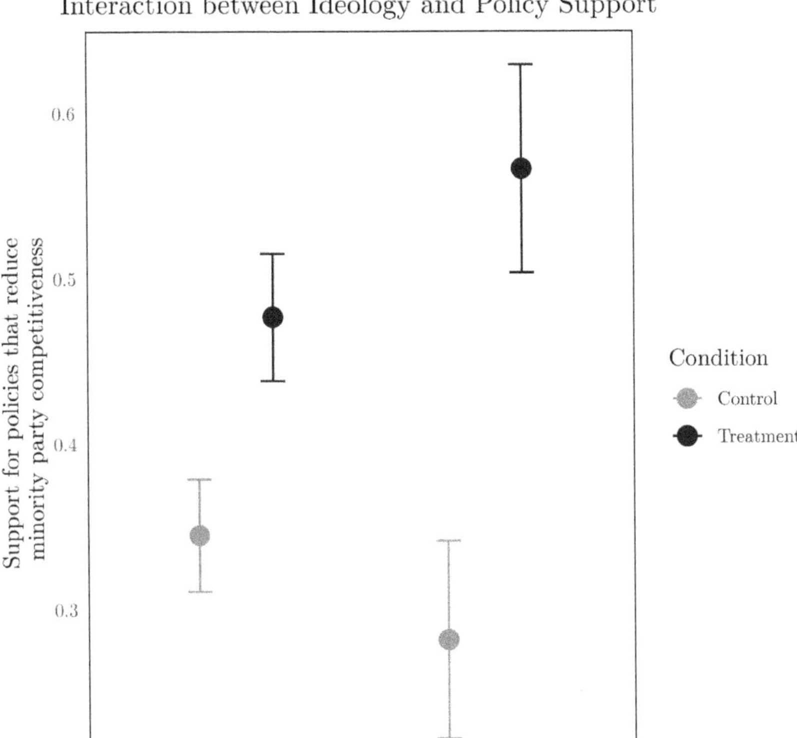

Figure 5 Interaction between strong ideological identification and response to treatment.

is "better to strike while the iron is hot" (Fiorina, 2017, p. 105). Political parties that find themselves temporarily out of power are also incentivized to oppose policies they might even believe would be good for the country, because they do not want their opponents in power to succeed.

CivicPulse provided data that linked respondents to their counties and the 2020 election results of those counties, allowing for an analysis of how political competition affects the willingness of respondents to subvert their opponents' power. I developed a simple measure of electoral competitiveness by calculating the absolute difference between the share of votes for Trump and Biden in a local policymaker's county in 2020. A lower number indicates greater competition, while a higher number suggests one-party dominance. Subtracting this value from one provides a continuous competitiveness measure, where 0 represents the least competitive counties and 1 the most competitive. Of course, it is likely that some counties voting heavily for Trump or Biden in 2020 were

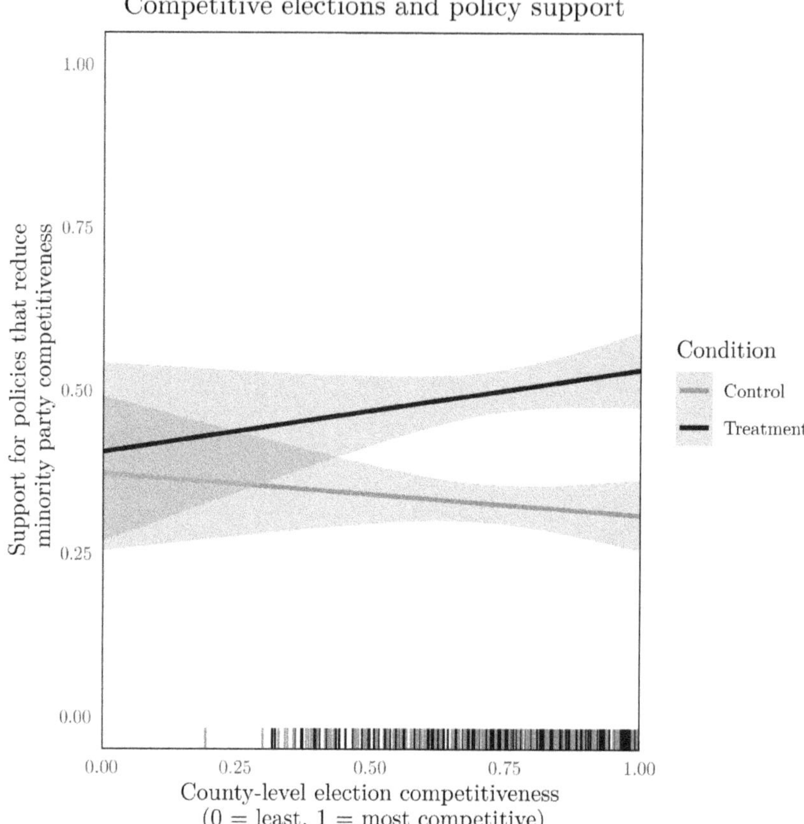

Figure 6 Interaction between election competitiveness across counties and response to treatment.

more balanced in their voting for local candidates, and these data cannot speak to that possibility.

Evaluating the interaction of this measure with treatment assignment (Figure 6) yields a nonsignificant result, with a *p*-value of 0.124. However, the direction aligns with the expectation that electoral competition motivates politicians to restrict their opponents' chances of victory or ability to influence policy.[26] These results imply that in the least competitive districts, treatment assignment has minimal impact on local elected leaders' policy support. Put differently, if a local official believes their victory or defeat is assured regardless of electoral rules, they seem to show little preference between policies that would enhance their reelection odds and those that would not. This makes sense

[26] Surprisingly, when evaluating the two policy scenarios separately, the one which manipulated the size of the board to reduce minority power accounts for the interaction between treatment and election competitiveness.

because when politicians view elections as uncompetitive due to their county's partisan makeup, they lack incentive to manipulate electoral rules or back policies that restrict partisan competition. As with the other analyses, the dependent variable averages responses to both policy scenarios.

Conversely, in the most competitive counties, politicians are about 19 percentage points more likely to support policies that restrict minority political rights when assigned to the treatment condition (and can be certain that their party will benefit). This pattern is logical: politicians facing especially narrow margins of victory or defeat may see favorable changes to electoral rules as a means to secure their power for years to come. Indeed, prior research indicates that electoral competition predicts the adoption of voter identification laws thought to reduce turnout among Democratic-leaning voters (Hicks et al., 2015; Hicks, McKee, & Smith, 2016). In competitive counties, even a tiny suppression of targeted demographics could decide outcomes. With that said, even as these counties with the most electoral competition may be the places with the most demand from politicians for anti-competitive reforms, because the votes are so close pulling off such reform may be especially difficult. Theoretically, the states where politicians will benefit from attempting to manipulate election results are the same states where doing so is most difficult because of robust political competition (Egorov & Sonin, 2023).

One notable limitation of exploring this interaction is that all policy scenarios were hypothetical, while the analysis draws on contextual data about respondents' actual political circumstances. Because these findings suggest that respondents considered their real-world political situations when evaluating hypothetical scenarios, this indicates incomplete compliance with experimental directions. When respondents followed instructions by fully abstracting from local conditions, this would bias the electoral competition analysis toward null results. Future research could present local leaders with custom-designed scenarios tailored to their specific districts (see Kalla and Porter (2021)).

4.3 Opponents Seem Threatening

Today's politicians are more ideological and face greater competition than in the past. Adding to these pressures is a third factor that may explain politicians' willingness to disregard democratic norms: the perceived threat from political opponents. Recent research argues that maintaining democratic competition resembles a "prisoner's dilemma game: if one party suspects the other is defecting, then the best response may be to defect" (Braley et al., 2023, p. 1,282). These authors argue that citizens who believe their opponents are subverting democracy will not hold their own leaders accountable for antidemocratic actions.

In this section, I extend this logic to politicians. In Section 3, I showed that both state legislators and local policymakers believed about 70% of their opponents would support policies that restrict minority political rights – a stark overestimation. Among the general public, people similarly overestimate the share of opponents willing to subvert democracy (Braley et al., 2023). Correcting these overestimates can reduce support for partisan violence (Mernyk et al., 2022). Together, these findings suggest that misperceptions about opponents may drive preemptive actions by politicians, who assume that losing power could prompt the other side to compromise democratic norms, perhaps even worse than they would, thus motivating them to restrict electoral competition as a precaution.

As in previous mechanism tests, I examined the interaction between treatment assignment and beliefs about the share of colleagues from the opposing party likely to support policies restricting minority rights. When politicians believe their opponents are highly likely to back these "bad" policies, they themselves support such policies 22% more frequently. Unlike in other mechanism tests, perceived threat from opponents was measured post-treatment, which complicates causal interpretation (Montgomery, Nyhan, & Torres, 2018). Figure 7 shows the results along with a distribution of perceived threat based on assignment to the control or treatment condition, with those in the treatment condition perceiving opponents as slightly more threatening.

This finding about the beliefs politicians develop about their political opponents challenges one explanation for the older theory of democratic elitism. Elitists argue that political experience prompts politicians to take a "sober second look" before undermining political norms (Sullivan et al., 1993, p. 53), believing that governing socializes politicians toward moderation and respect for opponents. Populists, by contrast, argue that governing reveals negative moral qualities in elites, seeing them as united across party lines in their desire to preserve their status (Urbinati, 2019, p. 63).

Testing these three mechanisms – strong ideological identification, political competition, and perceived threat from opponents – I found that each correlates with greater support for antidemocratic policies. Other mechanisms may also encourage support for restricting minority rights. For example, today's parties increasingly offer voters unified platforms nationwide (Hopkins, 2018, p. 10). In other words, Democrats in Ohio now propose similar policies as Democrats in New York. As state and local politics increasingly reflect national issues, state and local politicians may start viewing their colleagues and opponents as akin to the extreme federal legislators seen in the media. This homogenization

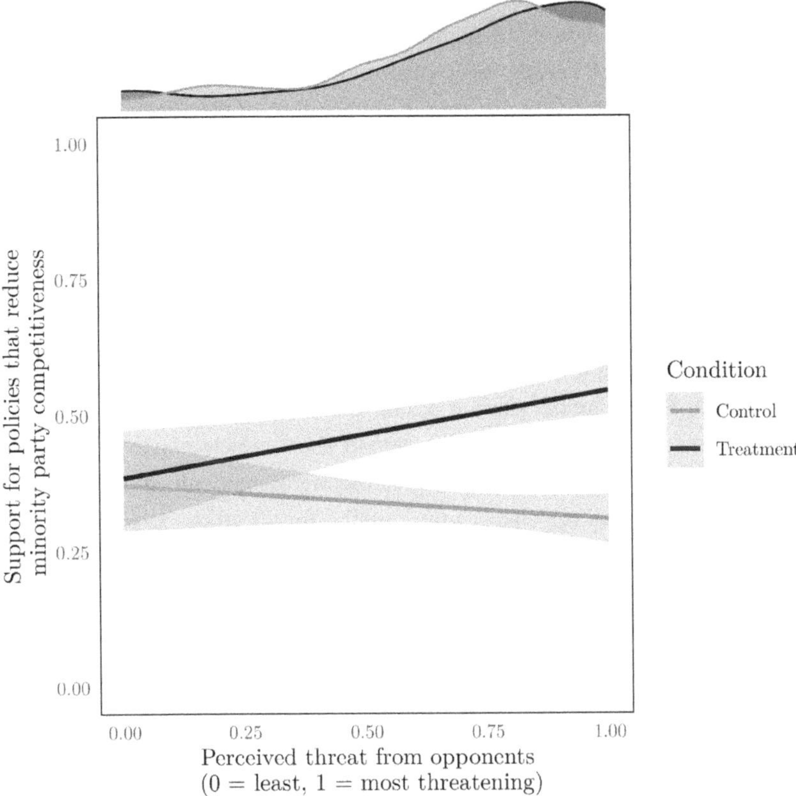

Figure 7 Distribution of opponents' expected antidemocratic policy support and that politicians who expect their opponents to support antidemocratic policies themselves respond more strongly to treatment. Perceived threat was measured after treatment which threatens any causal interpretation of these results (Montgomery et al., 2018).

of party platforms could further explain politicians' exaggerated pessimism about one another, and future work may explore that factor (and others) alongside the three that I have focused on here.

5 Acquiescence to Authoritarian Policies

The previous sections focused on experiments exploring unprincipled support for policies that make it harder for political minorities to contest elections or influence policy. In this section, I shift the focus from differential support for antidemocratic policies to politicians' attitudes toward fully authoritarian policies. Importantly, the results from these new studies highlight a nuanced dynamic: although politicians and members of the public generally reject blatant authoritarian measures, their resistance may weaken when democratic competition interferes with tangible partisan advantages.

The descriptive data that I reported in the second section of this Element were consistent with decades of research indicating that political elites support democratic principles at higher rates than members of the public. But the first set of experiments showed this to be questionable. What those experiments did not reveal was the extent of the antidemocratic policies that politicians might be willing to go along with. The four policy scenarios that I analyzed did not extend anywhere close to authoritarianism. After all, policies like gerrymandering and judicial manipulations are commonly proposed and enacted in American legislatures (J. Grumbach, 2022).

In another set of experiments, I tested whether politicians and the public are willing to tolerate the passing of outright authoritarian policies. This new design aimed to probe the limits of support for complete majoritarianism. In this set-up, I focus on an extreme form of majoritarian dominance – a one-time majority banning all opponents from running for all offices statewide. To do that, I use a conjoint experiment, which forces respondents to choose between randomized policy scenarios, to study hypothetical trade-offs in the minds of local elected leaders and the public. Respondents chose between two scenarios outlining potential states of the world, each detailing the outcome of the 2024 elections, an election law change enacted by the state legislature, and a salary adjustment also enacted by the state legislature.

Instead of focusing on respondents' support or opposition to specific policies, I examine their willingness to oppose antidemocratic policies when doing so is costly. Respondents were asked to evaluate extreme, clearly authoritarian policies within hypothetical scenarios, which removes ambiguity at the expense of the real-world relevance that I prioritized in the first design. With this second approach, I explore respondents' willingness to reject antidemocratic policies when such a stance comes with explicit costs.

One advantage of this approach is that, unlike the first set of more realistic studies, these experiments decouple support for these policies from direct electoral gains. Respondents can gain or lose control of their local governing board independent of whether the state legislature enacts an antidemocratic policy. This design allows us to observe politicians' potential willingness to acquiesce to such measures even when such support does not directly enhance their electoral success. Consequently, these results speak more to a generalized desire for one's own party to win than to any individual electoral performance.

The conjoint design incorporated four attributes: the 2024 presidential election outcome, the 2024 local election outcome, election legislation, and a salary adjustment. The election legislation attribute varied from a meaningless and harmless baseline (i.e., the state legislature recommending a nonbinding cap on campaign volunteers) to the blatantly authoritarian (i.e., the state legislature banning *all* opposing party members from running for any office statewide). This range simulates scenarios of total majority dominance, as respondents understand that their party would need legislative control to implement such extreme restrictions on competition.

Figure 8 illustrates an example of a conjoint trial scenario. In this case, the example respondent identifies as a Democrat. In Scenario A, Republicans have won the 2024 presidential election (an unfavorable outcome for the respondent), and the state legislature proposes a nonbinding cap on campaign volunteers (a neutral and meaningless policy change). In Scenario B, Democrats have secured the 2024 presidential victory (a favorable outcome for the respondent), and the state legislature enacts a policy banning all Republican candidates from state and local ballots. Given the design of this study, either party could win

It is important to remember that you might really like or dislike both scenarios, but we just want to learn which of the two you would choose.

	Scenario A	Scenario B
2024 National Election Outcome	Republicans win the Presidency but Congress is divided.	Democrats win the Presidency but Congress is divided.
2024 Local Election Outcome	Democrats take control of your local governing board.	Democrats take control of your local governing board.
Election Legislation	The state legislature recommends a non-binding cap on the number of campaign volunteers.	The state legislature bans all Republicans from competing in state and local campaigns in response to recent controversies.
Salary	Your employer raises your pay by 5%.	Your employer raises your pay by 10%.

Please tell us which of the two scenarios you prefer.

○ Scenario A

○ Scenario B

Figure 8 Example conjoint trial. In this example the respondent identifies as a Democrat. Either Republicans or Democrats can win upcoming national and local elections, but only Republicans can be banned from the ballot statewide.

upcoming elections, but only the respondent's political opponents face potential bans or restrictions on their competitive capacity.

I preregistered two hypotheses, which were that:[27]

- H1: Respondents will prefer scenarios in which their party wins the presidency / gains control of their local governing board.
- H2: Respondents are less likely to favor scenarios in which their party imposes restrictions on the ability of out-partisan candidates to run for office.

I expected that elected leaders would generally disfavor antidemocratic policies. At first glance, this might seem like a contradiction to the results of the veil-of-ignorance experiments designed to test politicians' principles. But it is essential to recall that in those experiments, even as the average treatment effects indicated partisan bias, most politicians still opposed antidemocratic policies that benefited their own side. Instead of looking for partisan hypocrisy in policy support, this conjoint design allows for a comparison between the strength of the preference for winning and the strength of the opposition to completely authoritarian policies.

As Sniderman recognized, elitists expect that politicians uphold democratic principles "even when they are contested" (Sniderman et al., 2000, p. 472). This concept of contestation suggests an inherent trade-off. The results from the first set of studies reveal that politicians may support policies based on unprincipled motivations, thus challenging the tenets of democratic elitism by examining the forces driving policy support. However, these studies stop short of probing the outer limits of politicians' willingness to abandon democratic norms. By introducing overtly authoritarian scenarios, the conjoint design addresses this gap, helping to identify the boundaries of politicians' tolerance for undemocratic actions when aligned with their interests.

I conducted this new experiment with local elected leaders in a second CivicPulse survey alongside a second general population sample for comparison purposes.[28] Table 6 shows the conjoint attributes alongside their levels. Note that in the actual studies "in-party" and "out-party" were replaced by the respondent's piped in party names. A Democrat would see Democrats for the in-party and Republicans for the out-party. The goal of this was to create scenarios that would be most relevant to the respondents.

---

[27] The preregistration is available at the OSF (https://osf.io/s4dm6). These studies were approved by the Institutional Review Board at the University of Texas at Dallas (IRB-24-272).

[28] I attempted to also recruit a second sample of state legislators to complete the conjoint task, but did not receive enough completed, usable responses (only 167), likely due to the increased length and complexity relative to the first experimental design.

Table 6 Conjoint attributes and levels. In the presentation to respondents, "in-party" and "out-party" were replaced by the respondents' piped in party names. A Democrat would see Democrats for the in-party and Republicans for the out-party.

Attribute	Levels
Presidential Election Outcome 2024	Out-party wins Presidency and takes control of Congress; out-party wins Presidency but Congress is divided; in-party wins Presidency but Congress is divided; in-party wins Presidency and takes control of Congress.
Local Election Outcome 2024	Out-party takes control of local governing board; Local governing board is evenly split; in-party takes control of local governing board.
Antidemocratic Legislation	Nonbinding cap on campaign volunteers; Restrict out-party candidate advertising; Ban out-party candidate from competing; Ban some out-party members from competing; Ban all out-party members from competing.
Salary Change	Pay unchanged; Pay cut by 20%; Pay cut by 10%; Pay cut by 5%; Pay raise by 5%; Pay raise by 10%; Pay raise by 20%.

5.1 Study 4: Local Elected Officials

For this study, 117 township, 290 municipal, and 95 county elected officials completed the survey. Comparing the median values from the respondent metadata with the sample frame again provides a benchmark to gauge representativeness. In this sample, the median respondent was from a county with a population of 8,340, with 26% having completed college, and 55% voting for Democrats. For comparison, the median population size of the sample frame is 5,830, with 22% college-educated, and a Democratic vote share of 58%. All responses used for analysis are from participants who self-identified as partisans (460 out of 502 respondents, with 255 Republican and 205 Democrat politicians). The survey began on February 23, 2024, and closed on April 8, 2024.

Due to timing constraints, I was unable to ask an extensive set of demographic questions of these respondents. However, of these respondents, about two-thirds faced a contested election the last time they ran for office. About 47% had worked in government before pursuing their political career. Because this was a conjoint experiment, each respondent completed three independently randomized trials. There were a total of 1,308 completed trials in this study (accounting for some respondents skipping questions).

I first report Average Marginal Component Effects (AMCEs), which measure how much a specific component of a conjoint scenario increases or decreases support for the policy scenario relative to a baseline, averaging across all other attributes (Hainmueller & Hopkins, 2015). Figure 9 shows that politicians are less likely to favor scenarios in which their political side bans candidates from the ballot. The AMCE for banning all opponents from all offices statewide is −20 percentage points, reassuringly indicating that respondents prefer to avoid restricting political competition. However, this preference is small compared to the preference for winning the 2024 presidential election. Politicians are about 57 percentage points more likely to choose scenarios in which their political side wins the presidency and control of Congress. Notably, respondents are largely indifferent to percentage salary changes, plausibly because many of these officials receive low salaries. This minimal weighting on personal compensation over democratic competition is a second reassuring finding.

To further explore support for authoritarian policies, I explicitly narrow the analysis to those 119 cases where the state legislature bans all out-party members from competing in all campaigns, and the in-party wins both the presidency and Congress. I calculated a selection probability of 65% for these scenarios. What this suggests is that the tension between partisan benefits and democratic principles – first identified in the mass public by Graham and Svolik (2020) – also checks politicians' defense of democracy. However, when evaluating these choices it is essential to recognize that even in this subset, 80% of the election legislation attributes were undemocratic. The only truly innocuous attribute was a nonbinding recommendation for a cap on campaign volunteers, meaning that in most scenarios, the alternative choice was also undemocratic, though much less so than a complete ban on opponents.

This fact that the baseline category for the democratic attributes was a nonbinding cap on campaign volunteers leads to another issue inherent to this conjoint analysis: all effects are interpreted relative to that baseline. Here, the nonbinding cap on volunteers was an unusual feature that may have been challenging for respondents to evaluate. If this attribute were a more straightforwardly pro-democratic or neutral but potentially more plausible choice, the negative effect of banning opposition members might appear stronger.

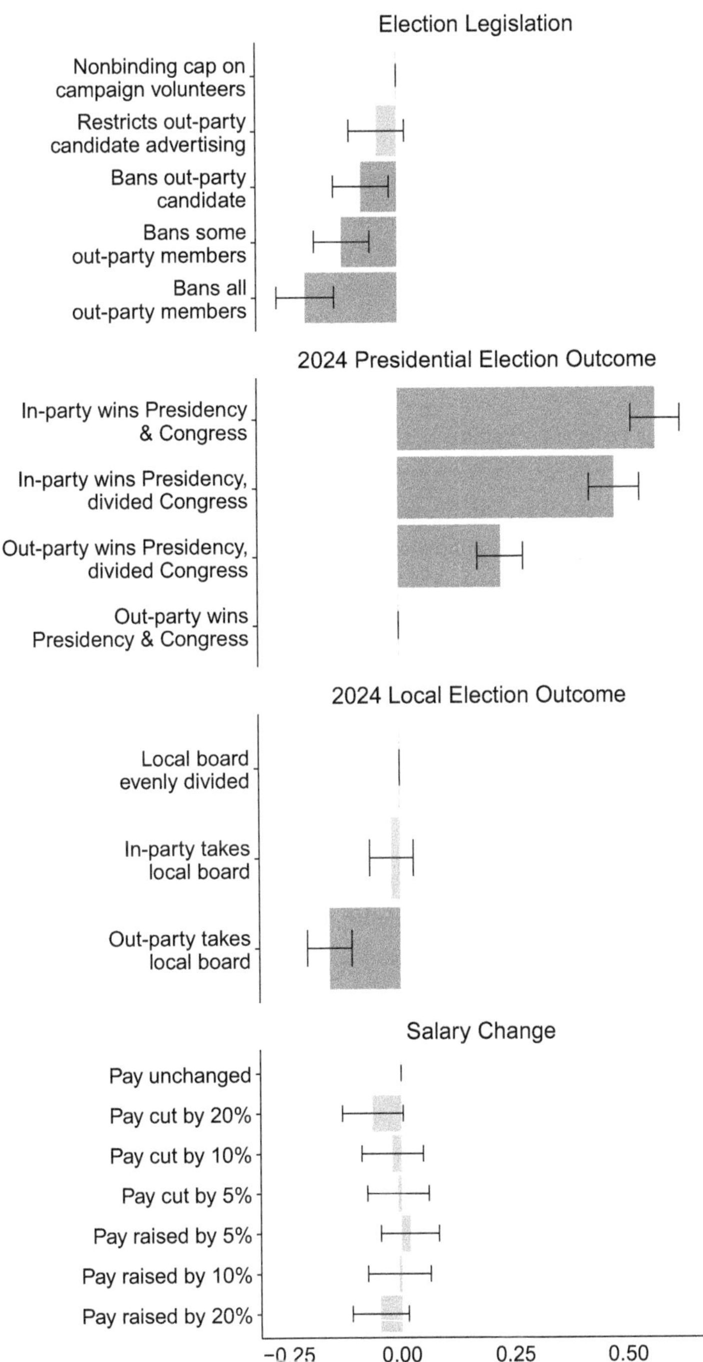

Figure 9 AMCEs for local elected leaders. Dark gray bars indicate results that are significantly different from the baseline at the 95% confidence level.

However, I intended the cap to seem essentially costless, as it was explicitly labeled as a recommendation for a nonbinding policy.

Still, AMCE and marginal means results are estimated considering the joint distribution of alternative possibilities. In this setup, the respondent is typically choosing from a menu of bad options with regard to democracy. But the other attributes have a much wider range of values (a complete victory or defeat in national elections, for example). Given the attribute levels are randomized independently, it is likely that the relative values a respondent places on levels of the election outcome attribute are more disparate than those placed on the election legislation attributes, challenging a comparison of such magnitudes.

Another potential reason for the muted effect of the democratic attribute could be respondents' perception of plausibility. Respondents might reasonably assume that a total ban on opposition parties would quickly be overturned in court. Outright bans on opposition parties are rare even in cases of democratic backsliding; more commonly, ruling parties modify electoral rules to disadvantage opponents without entirely eliminating competition (Levitsky & Ziblatt, 2019). Examples from Hungary and Turkey fit this model more closely than extreme cases like Venezuela, where even there the opposition is still not entirely banned. These inference limitations caution against an overly pessimistic interpretation of politicians' responses to these conjoint scenarios.

5.2 Study 5: General Public

I now turn to the comparison between general population respondents and those of politicians. The general population sample was recruited from CloudResearch's online, opt-in panel between February 12, 2024, and February 13, 2024. A total of 1,004 people completed the survey, and the final sample used for the analysis includes those 947 respondents who identified with either Democrats or Republicans, or those who stated that their views tend to be closer to one of the two major U.S. parties. I used quotas so that the sample approximately matches the population on observable demographics, though this step does not mean that the sample represents the population. Participants were evenly balanced between men and women. About 80% of the respondents self-identified as white, with 15% identified as Hispanic. There were 521 Democrats and 426 Republicans in the sample. Fifty-four percent of the participants claimed to have received a college or graduate degree.

Figure 10 shows the Average Marginal Component Effects (AMCE) results for this sample. The Online Appendix (Section 8.2) includes the full regression tables. People heavily favor scenarios in which their side wins the presidency.

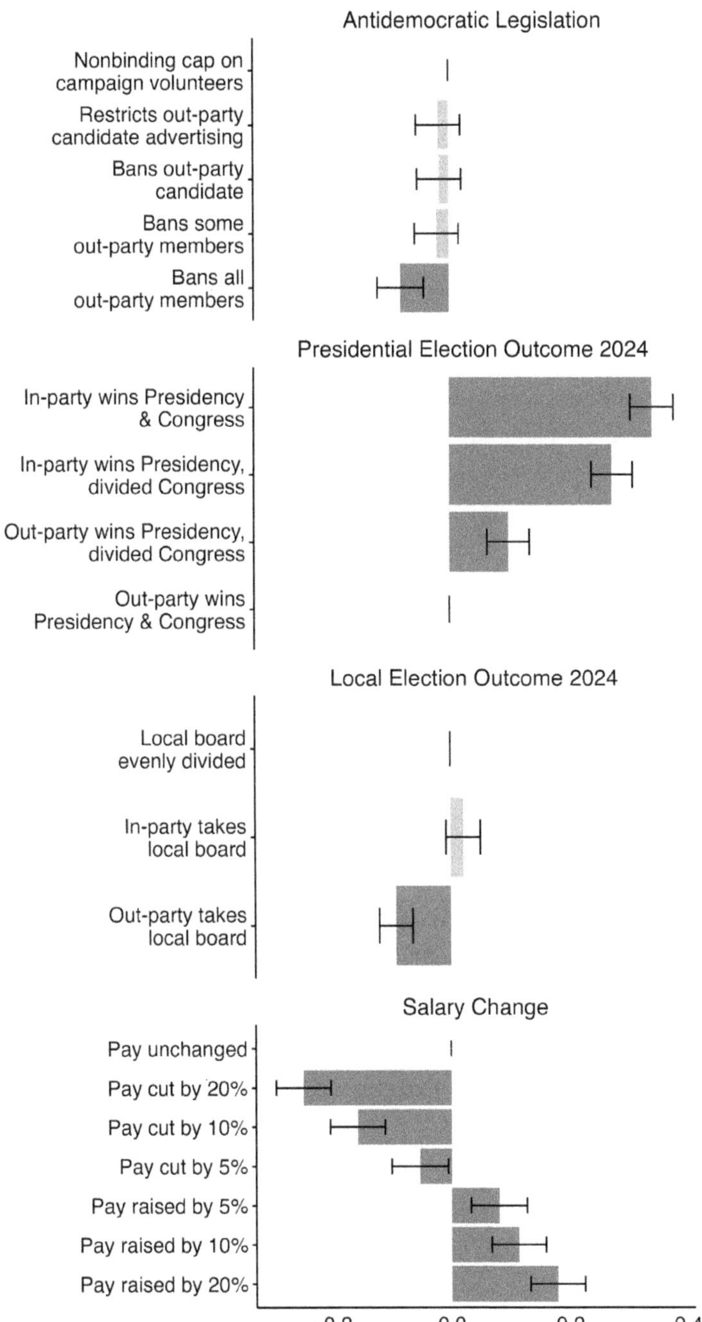

Figure 10 AMCE results for the general population. Dark gray bars indicate results that are significantly different from the baseline at the 95% confidence level.

People are 34 percentage points more likely to choose a scenario in which their side wins the 2024 presidential election and controls Congress. They are also 28 percentage points more likely to choose a scenario in which their preferred President wins in 2024 but Congress is divided. The relatively small difference between people's preferences for winning complete control of government and for divided Congress aligns with recent work finding that people are insensitive to the separation of powers (Bram, 2023a). The magnitude of the AMCEs for the 2024 election are substantively large and even exceed that of a 20% pay cut (−25 percentage points) or a 20% pay raise (18 percentage points).

Also, like elected leaders, public respondents are fairly insensitive to even flagrantly anti-democratic policies. There is no statistically significant penalty for restricting out-party advertising or banning one or some out-party candidates. Only when the state legislature decides to ban all out-party candidates do people avoid choosing the scenario, but the deterrent effect is just 8 percentage points.

Consistent with previous work (Druckman, Kang, et al., 2023a; Holliday et al., 2024) and with the earlier findings in this Element, local elected leaders and public respondents prefer not to enact antidemocratic policies in isolation. However, by shifting the focus to the opportunity costs of upholding democratic norms, I show that both elites and public respondents express some willingness to acquiesce to even flagrantly authoritarian policies. Specifically, respondents may have even placed more importance on their side winning the 2024 presidential election than on maintaining democratic political competition. These results imply that even if most politicians and most members of the public oppose measures that restrict political competition, politicians' strong preference for their side winning can cause some to tolerate the passage of antidemocratic policies.

5.3 How the Experiments Work Together

The two types of experiments each offer distinct strengths and weaknesses. By employing both designs, I aim to offset their respective limitations, allowing for a more comprehensive adjudication of elitist and populist theories. Several factors threaten the validity of the first set of veil-of-ignorance studies. First, the scenarios presented to respondents are relatively general, omitting important contextual details. For instance, asking respondents to consider hypothetical state legislators and local governments does not include specifics about the legislators' constituencies or the partisan composition of the legislative body. As a result, respondents are likely to project their own political contexts onto these hypothetical scenarios

Consider, for example, a scenario where respondents are asked to support a governor's appointment of a commission to draw legislative district boundaries, with the added information that "currently maps are drawn by a bipartisan commission." A respondent from a state like Massachusetts, where Democrats significantly outnumber Republicans, might view an evenly split bipartisan commission as disproportionately favorable to Republicans. In this case, a legislator may feel ambivalent about supporting partisan redistricting but could see it as more representative than the alternative – a commission evenly divided between Democrats and Republicans (Brunell, 2010).

The conjoint design overcomes the issue of local and statewide variation by introducing policies so extreme that partisan composition becomes nearly irrelevant. For instance, a policy banning all opposition candidates from running for office presents such a clear violation of democratic norms that, even in a strongly Democratic state like Massachusetts, it would be hard to justify as aligned with democratic principles.

A second limitation of the veil-of-ignorance experiments is that policies curbing minority power are fairly common in American legislatures (J. M. Grumbach, 2023). Partisan gerrymandering, for example, often leads to unequal vote weighting (Grofman, Koetzle, & Brunell, 1997). Reasonable people may disagree on whether partisan gerrymandering is inherently antidemocratic, and courts have issued varied rulings on the matter (Brunell, 2010, p. 84). The goal of these first three experiments was to separate principled policy support from partisan motivations without requiring agreement on which policies are definitively antidemocratic. Nonetheless, each policy scenario represented a significant shift from the status quo (Ahmed, 2023), moving in a less liberal-democratic direction.

This ambiguity regarding what constitutes democratic behavior is also linked to the fact that the veil-of-ignorance experiments specify the partisan affiliation of the bill's proponents. It is possible that respondents' loyalty to their party is not entirely unprincipled but instead reflects a belief that Democrats or Republicans are generally more likely to advocate effective policies. In such cases, support for antidemocratic policies may extend beyond partisan hypocrisy. Similarly, Sniderman contends that the "imperfect" alignment between professed principles and concrete choices does not necessarily indicate hypocrisy (Sniderman et al., 1996, p. 147). He argues that people often navigate multiple conflicting considerations, a view consistent with foundational perspectives on survey response patterns (Zaller & Feldman, 1992). Even when respondents' motivations may extend beyond mere partisan advantage, the conjoint experiment confronts them with the notion of banning all political opponents from running for office. This approach sidesteps debates about what qualifies as democratic or about biases toward policies proposed by particular parties.

Still, an unavoidable limitation for these types of hypothetical survey experiments is believability. The policy scenarios in the veil-of-ignorance studies depend on respondents accepting the effects described in the experiment. For instance, a Democratic legislator may find it implausible that switching from district to at-large elections would enhance their chances against Republicans. However, given the experimental nature of these scenarios, my primary concern was the variance between treatment and control conditions based on the specific information provided to respondents. Results could shift if respondents were exposed to additional or alternative information.

The conjoint experiment mitigates some of these contextual concerns while raising others. Unlike in the veil-of-ignorance studies, respondents in the conjoint are not asked to evaluate the potential effects of specific policies. Instead, they are choosing between scenarios without needing to believe in any subsequent political outcomes. For instance, banning all opponents from the ballot is simply presented as a given in these scenarios, making it fundamentally different from, say, switching to a new electoral system and being informed of hypothetical partisan advantages.

However, the conjoint design brings its own important believability challenges. Respondents may find it implausible that state legislators could feasibly ban an entire party from running. Additionally, they would certainly question the coherence of a scenario where a party is banned from the ballot yet retains control of a local governing board – a possible outcome in the experiment's design. These considerations highlight the importance of pairing the conjoint and veil-of-ignorance experiments. While the extreme scenarios in the conjoint design may strain credulity, the veil-of-ignorance studies resonate more closely with the real-world decisions that elected officials encounter.

What this means is that neither experimental design provides conclusive evidence due to the almost unavoidable trade-off between realism and clarity about what is or is not democratic. Taken together, these findings underscore that while individuals are reluctant to support antidemocratic policies, their commitment to democratic principles often weakens in the face of attainable partisan gains. In other words, the willingness to tolerate illiberal measures emerges not as a blanket endorsement of one party rule, but as a concession made when democratic ideals conflict with political expediency. Recognizing this conditionality reinforces the conclusion that the fixation of both elitists and populists on individual attitudes may overlook more promising institutional avenues for bolstering democratic resilience.

6 Democrats and Republicans Dislike Each Other, but Are Equally Self-serving

Democratic- and Republican-leaning citizens increasingly dislike and distrust their political opponents (Bakker & Lelkes, 2024; Druckman, Green, & Iyengar, 2023; Iyengar et al., 2019). One cause of this affective polarization is hostile rhetoric among political elites (Druckman et al., 2021). In this section, I first explore the attitudes of these elites toward each other, and toward the people they represent. I then consider any asymmetries in Democrats' and Republicans' responses to these experiments.

There is evidence that American political elites are even more affectively polarized than the public (Druckman & Levy, 2022; Enders, 2021). But this general phenomenon is not new; at least since the early 1990s, scholars have written about the decline in harmonious relationships in Congress (Uslaner, 1991, 1993). Politicians have noticed; one member of Congress said that "If we want Americans to be less divided at home, then we have to be less divided in Washington."[29]

At the end of the first CivicPulse survey of local policymakers, I asked these leaders to rate four groups on a 5-point scale. The groups were Democrat/Republican politicians and Democrat/Republican members of the public. Consistent with previous work, the difference in the ratings for regular American out-partisans was lower than the difference in ratings for out-partisan politicians (Druckman & Levendusky, 2019). That politicians have first-hand experience with their colleagues and yet still rate non-politicians more favorably suggests that elected officials might prefer serving in government if their polarized colleagues were replaced with members of the public. Figure 11 shows these results.

The 5-point scale shown in Figure 11 is different from the standard 0-100 scale researchers typically use to measure affective polarization. Rescaling these results, I find that in this sample the average difference in ratings between one's own party members and one's opposing party members is 39. The average difference in ratings between one's own side politicians and the politicians representing the other side is 42.

When researchers explore the extent of affective polarization between political parties, a key contributor is the overestimation of differences between political sides (Dorison, Minson, & Rogers, 2019; Westfall et al., 2015). What

[29] Perano, Ursula. "Republicans and Democrats in Congress Try to Be Friends Again-Sort of." The Daily Beast. December 12, 2022. Of course, positive relationships at the highest levels of government, like the U.S. Congress, are very different from those at relatively low levels, like the local- and state-level elected leaders in this study.

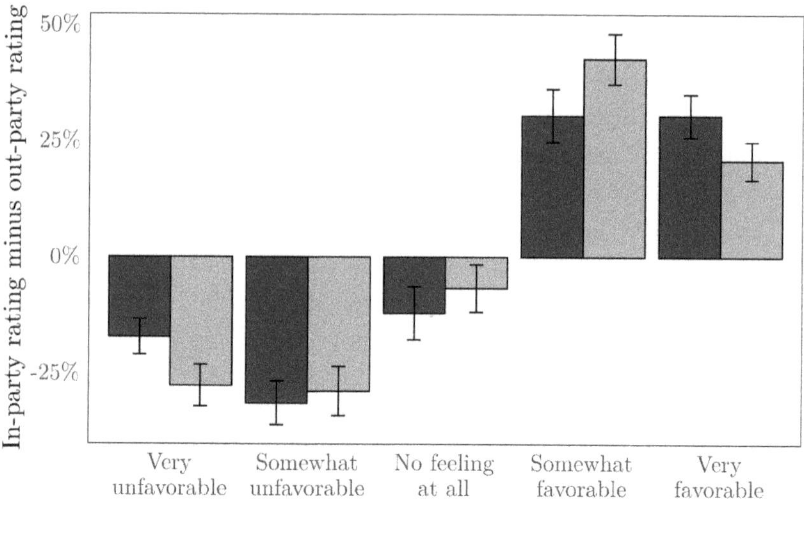

Figure 11 Local elected leaders' ratings for politicians and members of the public.

this means is that people believe that Republicans and Democrats are more different than they really are, and these biased perceptions increase partisan hostility (Bram, 2023b). These findings are consistent with those prior results.

In the previous sections, I found that state legislators and local policymakers incorrectly estimate that about 70% of their colleagues in the opposite party would support antidemocratic policies for partisan gain. Although politicians presumably know their colleagues well, state legislators and local elected leaders believe that their political opponents are much more likely to support policies that restrict minority political rights than those opponents actually are. I also showed that those beliefs about the threat posed by one's political opponents correlate with support for policies that restrict minority political rights. If partisans misperceive their opponents as more willing to subvert democratic principles than those opponents really are, then partisan hostility based on concerns about opponents' undermining democratic norms may be unjustified.[30]

This potential link between partisan hostility and the willingness to ignore democratic norms naturally leads to the question of whether such animosity is

[30] At the same time, recent research identifies mechanisms through which affective polarization itself undermines democratic norms (Kingzette et al., 2021). Still, others find that experimentally manipulating partisan hostility does not influence many political outcomes (Broockman, Kalla, & Westwood, 2023).

justified. If either Democrats or Republicans are systematically more or less committed to democratic principles, then that would seem to validate partisan dislike for each other. For example, if Democrats would never give up on our democratic system, but Republicans would, then Democrats would have additional reasons for disliking Republicans. In a further analysis, I explore any differences in how Republicans and Democrats respond to treatment in all experiments reported in this Element.

There are reasons to expect partisan asymmetries – with research indicating that Republican control at the state level correlates with democratic backsliding (J. Grumbach, 2022). Furthermore, scholars of democratic backsliding have focused their attention on Republican political elites (L. M. Bartels & Carnes, 2023; Hacker & Pierson, 2015). Even before the Trump presidency, researchers have critiqued the most straightforward version of democratic elitism by looking at variation between elites themselves, and not just between elites and the public. For example, Sniderman and colleagues reanalyzed McClosky's data (Sniderman et al., 1991). These authors found evidence that, even though McClosky identified a higher average level of support for democratic norms among political elites than among the mass public, there was meaningful variation. Specifically, conservative political elites were less supportive of democratic norms than liberal citizens (Sniderman et al., 1991, p. 365). More recently, some have argued that Republicans among the mass public may be less committed to democratic norms than Democrats (L. M. Bartels, 2020; de Oliveira Santos & Jost, 2024).[31]

Those findings motivate additional analysis to understand whether Democrats or Republicans respond differently to these experiments (Table 7). I tested for an interaction between treatment assignment and Republican party identification in all three partisan veil-of-ignorance studies. All respondents in the analysis for these experiments were Democrats or Republicans, and I found no evidence that members of either party are more responsive to treatment, whether looking at state legislators, local elected leaders, or members of the public. Sniderman and colleagues lay the blame on the right, but today it seems to be politicians from both parties who, when given an explicit choice, prioritize their partisan interests.

These results indicate that neither Democrats nor Republicans are justified in thinking that the other is less dedicated to democratic principles. What about any potential differences in acquiescence to authoritarian policies? When turning to the conjoint experiment examining authoritarian policy

[31] At the same time, other work finds no difference in motivated reasoning between Democrats and Republicans (Guay & Johnston, 2022).

Table 7 Testing for an interaction between partisanship and treatment assignment.

	Policy Support Across Samples		
	State Legislators	**Local Policymakers**	**General Public**
Treatment	0.164^{***}	0.181^{***}	0.125^{***}
	(0.038)	(0.033)	(0.012)
Republican	0.113^{*}	0.002	−0.004
	(0.047)	(0.032)	(0.014)
Treatment	−0.099	−0.024	−0.013
× Republican	(0.062)	(0.045)	(0.012)
Intercept	0.294^{***}	0.330^{***}	0.448^{***}
	(0.031)	(0.024)	(0.013)
Observations	511	427	3,316
R^2	0.054	0.118	0.055
Adjusted R^2	0.047	0.112	0.053

$^{*}p < 0.1$; $^{**}p < 0.05$; $^{***}p < 0.01$

scenarios, it is necessary to move past AMCEs to explore partisan asymmetries. AMCEs are useful for analyzing the causal effects of different attribute levels on respondent choices, but do not allow for comparisons of how different groups of respondents react to the scenarios. In a new analysis of the second local elected leader study, I report conditional marginal means for Republican and Democrat respondents (Figure 12). Marginal means reveal the percentage of time that a scenario is selected when a given attribute level is included (Leeper, Hobolt, & Tilley, 2020). Democrats selected scenarios in which Democrats win the next presidential election and control Congress 76% of the time; Republicans selected scenarios in which Republicans win 75% of the time.

Turning to the general population sample, marginal means analysis does suggest that Democrats may be slightly more averse to banning Republicans from running for office than Republicans are from banning Democrats (see the Online Appendix Section 8.4). This suggests that there may be some justification for thinking that Republican members of the public are less committed to democratic norms, but I only find that result in one of five studies reported in this Element and only in a nonrepresentative general population sample.

The absence of any partisan asymmetry in the elite studies suggests a path for strengthening democratic attitudes among politicians. Other experimental evidence shows that it is possible to reduce the support of state legislators for

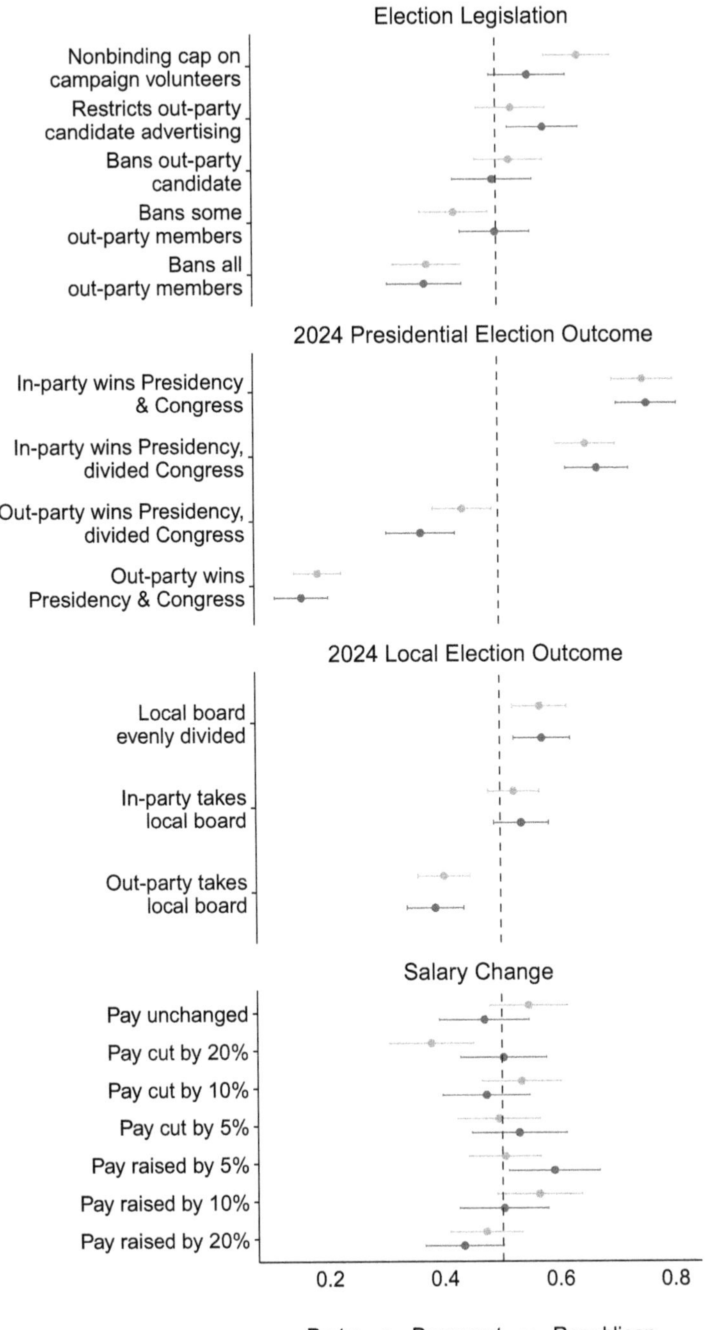

Figure 12 Conditional marginal means for Democrat and Republican elected leaders.

antidemocratic policies by providing information on public opposition to such policies (Druckman, Kang, et al., 2023a).[32] That study found that legislators have fairly accurate views of their own side. But in a departure from those results, one additional finding from these experiments is that politicians do not just overestimate the antidemocratic tendencies of their opponents, they also overestimate how willing their colleagues would be to restrict minority political rights. This finding suggests that politicians may go along with antidemocratic bills to remain in the good graces of colleagues putting forward such policies on their own side. Such "bandwagoning" occurs when elites within a coalition acquiesce to antidemocratic practices (Pierson & Schickler, 2020, p. 53).

Many politicians may want to take a sober second look at policies, but they believe that their opponents will not, and so they cannot respect democratic norms themselves. These beliefs about colleagues may be causing something akin to a preemptive strike on the other side, where politicians are more willing to deny political power to their opponents out of fear for the future. If politicians can work with their colleagues to ensure that future majorities will not restrict political competition, then both sides may be able to avoid striking first, confident that they will be able to effectively contest upcoming elections.

7 "How Did That Happen?"

In this Element, I have argued that contemporary critics of populism and past scholars of democratic elitism share an empirical question: who is more committed to democratic principles, the public or the elites? Five experiments conducted with members of the public, local elected leaders, and sitting state legislators indicate a dual threat to American democracy – both elites and the public demonstrate a hypocritical willingness to manipulate elections and restrict minority political rights. All five studies indicate that for some, holding onto political power is more important than supporting fair political competition.

As Robert Dahl observed over fifty years ago, empirical evidence on American attitudes toward civil liberties often reveals "considerably less than a widespread and confident commitment to democratic and libertarian norms" (Dahl, 1966, p. 299). Yet, despite this ambivalence, Dahl highlighted the paradox that antidemocratic policy opinions are not more frequently transmuted into national policy, crediting the resilience of the Supreme Court and other liberal-institutional safeguards. These findings reaffirm Dahl's conclusion because even as I find that both elites and the public exhibit conditional

[32] However, still more recent work finds that competitive information undermines the effect of correcting misperceptions (Druckman, Kang, et al., 2023b).

support for democratic principles, institutions continue to act as crucial buffers against the impulses of pure majoritarianism and the resulting partisan excess. These results suggest that the stability of American democracy depends less on the principled behavior of individuals and more on the robustness of its institutions, many of which, even in an era of polarization, continue to uphold the foundational commitments to fair political competition and minority rights.

Still, the findings accompany rising political polarization (Abramowitz & McCoy, 2019; McCoy, Rahman, & Somer, 2018), which motivates more extreme politicians to appeal to more extreme constituents (Merrill, Grofman, & Brunell, 2022). What can be done? One promising idea is to work to change the composition of those who enter office. Democratic elitists suggested that serving in office would moderate the views of politicians. In the first set of veil-of-ignorance studies, I found that less ideological politicians were less likely to support antidemocratic policies than strong ideologues on the left and right. If moderate candidates can run and win elections, even as partisans, then they may be able to work with colleagues across the aisle to support fair political competition. This idea is consistent with previous work that found that among the public, moderates punish politicians for antidemocratic behavior (Graham & Svolik, 2020, p. 383).

Although more moderate politicians may help to check the attitudes of some extremist colleagues, attitudinal or compositional interventions will likely only take us so far. Ultimately, strong institutional safeguards are essential for maintaining democratic competition. In earlier sections, I quoted the authors of the U.S. Constitution. Those thinkers recognized that people are self-interested, that we need institutions to check ambition, and that partisanship is dangerous for liberal democracy.

Perhaps the clearest statement comes from Madison, who said, "If the impulse and the opportunity be suffered to coincide, we well know that neither moral nor religious motives can be relied on as an adequate control" (Madison, 1787). Madison's concerns align closely with these findings, emphasizing the need for institutional checks on politicians' self-interested behavior. He is saying that values are not enough; it is important that formal rules withhold the opportunity to subvert democratic competition. Yet for decades democratic elitists thought that politicians would be the ones to "restrain the passions of the public" (Sniderman et al., 1996, p. 18). Today's critics of populism may place high expectations on non-populist leaders to uphold democratic norms, yet these results suggest that the inclination to prioritize partisan advantages is more widespread, extending across party lines.

These findings naturally raise the question of why today's elites are losing credibility with the public. Although the old theory of democratic elitism does not receive much attention from scholars or the public,[33] the underlying idea that politicians and other elites are "better" in some important way is alive and well. Widely read books describe the "Death of Expertise" (Nichols, 2017). Some puzzle over the fact that public trust in the federal government has declined from a high of 77% in 1964 to just 16% in 2023.[34] During the Covid-19 pandemic, there were countless calls for more attention to and compliance with the views of public health experts.

Any speculation about the causes of the decline in trust in elites must grapple with the possibility that many elites are not particularly trustworthy. Machiavelli famously said that "The nature of the masses, then, is no more reprehensible than is the nature of princes, for all do wrong and to the same extent when there is nothing to prevent them doing wrong." Of course, this is difficult to assess. The results in this Element come from one-shot experiments conducted at a single moment in time with state legislators and local elected leaders, and cannot directly address the question of whether elites today really are less principled than those of the past. Still, these experiments challenge the assumptions of elitist theories of democracy, suggesting those assumptions do not hold for today's politicians. And one cause of the decline in trust in elites and the accompanying rise of populism is very likely this failure of elites to take consistent and principled positions on policies.

Elite failure has led even harsh critics of populism to recognize that there is at least some truth to populist complaints. After all, populism is an "illiberal," but still democratic, response to "undemocratic liberalism" (Mudde & Rovira Kaltwasser, 2018, p. 1,670). What this means is that populists respond to factors that include the transfer of power to unelected bureaucrats and the general lack of elite responsiveness to popular demands (Berman, 2021, pp. 79–80). Some argue that the rise of nonmajoritarian institutions really has reduced the responsiveness of political institutions, which populists now see as nearly impossible to influence through regular channels of politics (Zürn, 2022, p. 790). Theorists since Schumpeter have suggested that the tension between "democratic ideals and liberal representative practice imposes on the masses and elites a burden so great that the system might collapse" (Piano, 2019, p. 532).

I have focused these experiments on electoral politics, with samples of elected politicians answering questions about respect for minority political rights and the opportunity to contest elections. But the tension between elites'

[33] But see: Best and Higley (2018); Higley and Burton (2006).
[34] "Public Trust in Government: 1958–2023." Pew Research. September 19, 2023.

professed ideals and reality extends much further. A core populist accusation is that of widespread elite hypocrisy (Furia, 2009; Mangset et al., 2019). Those charges extend far beyond the treatment of political opponents to include politicians' day-to-day behavior.[35]

In a striking and substantively significant example that revealed widespread hypocrisy among elites, think back to the height of the Covid-19 pandemic. A *Washington Post* columnist wrote that the "The pandemic took the worst hypocrisies of each party – and made them worse."[36] For example, Democratic politicians and many medical experts advocated strict social distancing, but then completely reversed themselves when protests for racial justice broke out.[37] California Governor Gavin Newsom attended a celebratory dinner while other restaurants were closed,[38] and kept his children in an in-person private school while public school children were at home.[39] On the other side, Trump and his allies like Rudy Giuliani received special treatments that were in short supply, even as they downplayed the seriousness of the pandemic.[40] Prominent Republicans also "railed against mask mandates" but then complied "when no one is paying attention."[41]

Perhaps the clearest example of elite hypocrisy started not with politicians but with some members of the scientific community. In March 2020, twenty-seven scientists published a letter in the medical journal *The Lancet*, writing that "We stand together to strongly condemn conspiracy theories suggesting that COVID-19 does not have a natural origin" (Calisher et al., 2020, p. e42). The problem is that they lacked evidence to make such a strong claim and later had to add a conflict of interest declaration to their statement (Lenharo & Wolf, 2024). Their position that it was a conspiracy theory to even raise the possibility of a lab leak was not at all justified by evidence, and in taking such a strong stance without good reasons, they had a meaningful negative impact on the critically important public conversation about the origins of Covid-19.

---

35 For example, "populist commentators on the political right took much glee in observing that John Kerry, although an avowed environmentalist, apparently owned at least three sport utility vehicles" (Furia, 2009, p. 121).

36 McArdle, Megan. "The pandemic took the worst hypocrisies of each party – and made them worse." The Washington Post. December 16, 2020.

37 Simon, Mallory. "Over 1,000 health professionals sign a letter saying, Don't shut down protests using coronavirus concerns as an excuse." CNN. June 5, 2020.

38 Armus, Teo. "California Democrats urged people to stay home – and then did the opposite at restaurants and holiday parties." The Washington Post. December 2, 2020.

39 Mays, Mackenzie. "Newsom sends his children back to private school classrooms in California." Politico. October 30, 2020.

40 Gay Stolberg, Sheryl. "Trump and Friends Got Coronavirus Care Many Others Couldn't." The New York Times. December 9, 2020.

41 Lemon, Jason. "Ilhan Omar Calls Marjorie Taylor Greene 'Hypocrite Cult Leader' Over Masked Airplane Photo." Newsweek. September 18, 2021.

Because these scientists had come out so strongly in favor of the natural origins hypothesis, media sources followed. In September 2020 PolitiFact called the lab-leak hypothesis a "debunked conspiracy theory" and described a FoxNews guest sharing the hypothesis as spreading a claim that is "inaccurate and ridiculous. We rate it Pants on Fire!"[42] Of course, the lab leak hypothesis was never a debunked conspiracy theory; it was just labeled as such by a select group of scientists who, with the advantage of hindsight, now appear to have been acting in their own self-interest. Even at the time of this writing, four years later, debate continues over whether Covid-19 originated in a lab or in the wild.[43]

We cannot yet be certain of the origins of the virus, but what is certain is that media organizations were labeling the lab leak hypothesis as a debunked conspiracy theory when they had not even bothered to gather any systematic evidence about the beliefs of scientists. In July 2021, well before the current near-universal acknowledgment that a lab leak is plausible, I contacted 1,421 researchers at the US-News ranked top 25 microbiology (including virology and immunology) departments in the world. I asked them to take a short survey. The aim of this survey was to give many scientists the opportunity to share their opinion about where Covid-19 came from.[44]

I asked them what they think is the likelihood that the virus that causes Covid-19 was first introduced to humans after a laboratory incident. Ninety-eight responded, and on average, they said that there was a 27% chance that the pandemic was the result of a laboratory incident. Very few respondents completely dismissed the lab leak hypothesis: just seven believed that there was a 0% chance that the virus originated in a laboratory, and only 27 reported a less than 10% chance. Only six claimed a greater than 75% chance that the lab leak hypothesis was true, fewer than the number of researchers who completely dismissed the possibility.

If PolitiFact and other media organizations had wanted to fairly and reasonably set the agenda for discussing the lab leak hypothesis, then they and other fact-checkers could have attempted a similar survey instead of just listening to a handful of plausibly conflicted scientists. Expert surveys like this may be one way to rebuild trust in elites. Such anonymous surveys will likely reveal important variation. That variation reflects genuine uncertainty about the world and

---

42 Funke, Daniel. "Tucker Carlson guest airs debunked conspiracy theory that COVID-19 was created in a lab." PolitiFact. September 16, 2020.

43 Marquardt, Alex and Cohen, Zachary. "US intel community still believes Covid-19 could have originated from lab or in wild." CNN. June 23, 2023.

44 That study was approved by Duke University's Institutional Review Board (protocol # 2022–0022).

the fact that, like the issue of what is or is not democratic, reasonable people can and will disagree over almost anything. This disagreement is not just about different values. Instead, disagreement often reflects real ambiguities in data and matters of fact, as in the example of the origins of Covid-19. It is essential to recognize and accept this uncertainty. One important and often overlooked benefit of doing so is that by accepting the reality of uncertainty, politicians and other elites can avoid having to reverse themselves, as they often have in recent years.

This pattern of elites maintaining near certainty in something, before later reversing themselves, extends far beyond the Covid-19 pandemic (Bram, 2021). For example, and to return to electoral politics and the story that opened this Element, two straightforward cases of elite reversals are Lindsey Graham's and Joe Biden's attitudes toward election-year Supreme Court confirmations. Both Biden and Graham acted as if their initial opposition to confirming new justices in an election year was based on timeless principles. Lindsey Graham specifically said that regardless of what happened in the future, he would stick to it. But what the introduction left out is what Graham said once he reversed himself and voted to confirm a conservative to the court in an election year. He attempted to justify his reversal as

> a direct response to Democrats' attempts to weaponize the judicial confirmation process, first by doing away with the filibuster that allowed a minority to block lower-court judicial nominees, and then by stridently opposing Justice Brett M. Kavanaugh's nomination in 2018 during a heated confirmation battle.[45]

Of course, Graham's justification is a stretch. But regardless of its merits, the case Graham tried to make is that the world had changed since he made his original statement promising to reject election-year nominees. In this, Graham is right. The world is always changing, and politicians and other elites will have to respond to those changes. If he had not initially made such a strong reference to timeless principles that he did not really think were so timeless back in 2016, he would not have had to reverse himself in 2020. Similarly, if PolitiFact had not made such an aggressive attempt to subvert discussion of the lab leak hypothesis, they would not have had to reverse themselves when their position became untenable. This points to a potential strategy for elites aiming to rebuild trust. Those wishing to bolster their credibility can be more open to the possibility that the world can and will change.

---

45 Edmondson, Catie. "'You Would Do the Same': Graham is Defiant on Supreme Court Reversal." The New York Times. September 21, 2020.

Jon Stewart made a compelling case for elite open-mindedness in a June 2021 appearance on *The Late Show* with Stephen Colbert.[46] He started by recognizing the uncertainty immediately after the initial Covid outbreak: "There's a novel respiratory coronavirus overtaking Wuhan, China, what do we do?" Then, with a mix of humor and common sense, he suggested investigating what happened at the Wuhan Institute of Virology: "Oh, you know who we could ask? The Wuhan novel respiratory coronavirus lab. The disease is the same name as the lab." Stewart's approach was simple: "That's just a little too weird, don't you think? Look at the name! Show me your business card! Oh, I work at the coronavirus lab in Wuhan. Oh, there's a coronavirus loose in Wuhan." Finally, he asked: "How did that happen?"

[46] Ivie, Devon. "Jon Stewart Wants You to 'Stop With the Logic' and Accept His Lab-Leak Theory." New York Magazine / Vulture. June 15, 2021.

References

Abramowitz, A., & McCoy, J. (2019). United States: Racial resentment, negative partisanship, and polarization in Trump's America. *The ANNALS of the American Academy of Political and Social Science*, *681*(1), 137–156.

Ahmed, A. (2023). Is the American public really turning away from democracy? backsliding and the conceptual challenges of understanding public attitudes. *Perspectives on Politics*, *21*(3), 967–978.

Akkerman, A., Mudde, C., & Zaslove, A. (2014). How populist are the people? measuring populist attitudes in voters. *Comparative Political Studies*, *47*(9), 1324–1353.

Algara, C., & Johnston, S. (2022). The rising electoral role of polarization & implications for policymaking in the United States Senate: Assessing the consequences of polarization in the senate from 1914–2020. In *The forum* (Vol. 19, no. 4, pp. 549–583). https://doi.org/10.1515/for-2021-2034.

Amlani, S., & Algara, C. (2021). Partisanship & nationalization in American elections: Evidence from presidential, senatorial, & gubernatorial elections in the US counties, 1872–2020. *Electoral Studies*, *73*, 102387.

Anzia, S. F. (2021). Party and ideology in American local government: An appraisal. *Annual Review of Political Science*, *24*, 133–150.

Bakker, B. N., & Lelkes, Y. (2024). Putting the affect into affective polarisation. *Cognition and Emotion*, *38*(4), 418–436. https://doi.org/10.1080/02699931.2024.2362366.

Bartels, B. L., & Johnston, C. D. (2020). *Curbing the court: Why the public constrains judicial independence*. Cambridge University Press.

Bartels, L. M. (2020). Ethnic antagonism erodes republicans' commitment to democracy. *Proceedings of the National Academy of Sciences*, *117*(37), 22752–22759.

Bartels, L. M., & Carnes, N. (2023). House republicans were rewarded for supporting Donald Trump's "stop the steal" efforts. *Proceedings of the National Academy of Sciences*, *120*(34), e2309072120.

Bartels, L. M., Daxecker, U. E., Hyde, S. D. et al. (2023). The forum: Global challenges to democracy? perspectives on democratic backsliding. *International Studies Review*, *25*(2), viad019.

Berman, S. (2021). The causes of populism in the west. *Annual Review of Political Science*, *24*, 71–88.

Bermeo, N. (2016). On democratic backsliding. *Journal of Democracy*, *27*, 5.

Besley, T., & Coate, S. (1997). An economic model of representative democracy. *The Quarterly Journal of Economics*, *112*(1), 85–114.

Best, H., & Higley, J. (2018). *The Palgrave handbook of political elites: Introduction*. Springer.

Braley, A., Lenz, G. S., Adjodah, D., Rahnama, H., & Pentland, A. (2023). Why voters who value democracy participate in democratic backsliding. *Nature Human Behaviour*, *7*, 1282–1293. https://doi.org/10.1038/s41562-023-01594-w.

Bram, C. (2021). When a conspiracy theory goes mainstream, people feel more positive toward conspiracy theorists. *Research & Politics*, *8*(4), 20531680211067640.

Bram, C. (2023a). Expectations for policy change and participation. *Public Opinion Quarterly*, *87*(4), 1000–1012.

Bram, C. (2023b). The most important election of our lifetime: Focalism and political participation. *Political Psychology*, *44*(5), 943–960.

Bram, C. (2024). Beyond partisan filters: Can underreported news reduce issue polarization? *Plos One*, *19*(2), e0297808.

Broockman, D. E., Kalla, J. L., & Westwood, S. J. (2023). Does affective polarization undermine democratic norms or accountability? maybe not. *American Journal of Political Science*, *67*, 808–828. https://doi.org/10.1111/ajps.12719.

Brunell, T. (2010). *Redistricting and representation: Why competitive elections are bad for America*. Routledge.

Calisher, C., Carroll, D., Colwell, R. et al. (2020). Statement in support of the scientists, public health professionals, and medical professionals of china combatting covid-19. *The Lancet*, *395*(10226), e42–e43.

Carey, J., Clayton, K., Helmke, G. et al. (2022). Who will defend democracy? evaluating tradeoffs in candidate support among partisan donors and voters. *Journal of Elections, Public Opinion and Parties*, *32*(1), 230–245.

Carnes, N. (2013). *White-collar government: The hidden role of class in economic policy making*. University of Chicago Press.

Chang, L., & Krosnick, J. A. (2009). National surveys via RDD telephone interviewing versus the internet: Comparing sample representativeness and response quality. *Public Opinion Quarterly*, *73*(4), 641–678.

Cheruvu, S. (2023). Education, public support for institutions, and the separation of powers. *Political Science Research and Methods*, *11*(3), 570–587. https://doi.org/10.1017/psrm.2022.29.

Clayton, K. (2023). Understanding public attitudes toward restrictive voting laws in the United States. *Research & Politics*, *10*(4), 20531680231206611.

Dahl, R. A. (1966). Further reflections on “the elitist theory of democracy.” *American Political Science Review*, *60*(2), 296–305.

de Oliveira Santos, D., & Jost, J. T. (2024). Liberal-conservative asymmetries in anti-democratic tendencies are partly explained by psychological differences in a nationally representative US sample. *Communications Psychology*, *2*(1). https://doi.org/10.1038/s44271-024-00096-3.

Dorison, C. A., Minson, J. A., & Rogers, T. (2019). Selective exposure partly relies on faulty affective forecasts. *Cognition*, *188*, 98–107.

Druckman, J. N., & Bolsen, T. (2011). Framing, motivated reasoning, and opinions about emergent technologies. *Journal of Communication*, *61*(4), 659–688.

Druckman, J. N., Green, D. P., & Iyengar, S. (2023). Does affective polarization contribute to democratic backsliding in America? *The ANNALS of the American Academy of Political and Social Science*, *708*(1), 137–163.

Druckman, J. N., Kang, S., Chu, J. et al. (2023a). Correcting misperceptions of out-partisans decreases American legislators’ support for undemocratic practices. *Proceedings of the National Academy of Sciences*, *120*(23), e2301836120.

Druckman, J. N., Kang, S., Chu, J. et al. (2023b). Correcting misperceptions of out-partisans decreases American legislators’ support for undemocratic practices. *Proceedings of the National Academy of Sciences*, *120*(23), e2301836120.

Druckman, J. N., Klar, S., Krupnikov, Y., Levendusky, M., & Ryan, J. B. (2021). Affective polarization, local contexts and public opinion in America. *Nature Human Behaviour*, *5*(1), 28–38.

Druckman, J. N., & Levendusky, M. S. (2019). What Do We Measure When We Measure Affective Polarization? *Public Opinion Quarterly*, *83*(1), 114–122. https://doi.org/10.1093/poq/nfz003.

Druckman, J. N., & Levy, J. (2022). Affective polarization in the American public. In Thomas Rudolph, ed., *Handbook on politics and public opinion* (pp. 257–270). Edward Elgar.

Druckman, J. N., Peterson, E., & Slothuus, R. (2013). How elite partisan polarization affects public opinion formation. *Solutions to Political Polarization in America*, *107*(1), 57–79.

Eggers, A. C. (2014). Partisanship and electoral accountability: Evidence from the UK expenses scandal. *Quarterly Journal of Political Science*, *9*(4), 441–472.

Egorov, G., & Sonin, K. (2023). Electoral college and election fraud. *National Bureau of Economic Research.*

Elster, J. (1994). Die schaffung von verfassungen: Analyse der allgemeinen grundlagen. *Zum Begriff der Verfassung. Die Ordnung des Politischen, Frankfurt a. M*, 37–57.

Enders, A. M. (2021). Issues versus affect: How do elite and mass polarization compare? *The Journal of Politics*, *83*(4), 1872–1877.

Fiorina, M. P. (2017). *Unstable majorities: Polarization, party sorting, and political stalemate*. Hoover press.

Flanders, C. (2012). Election law behind a veil of ignorance. *Florida Law Review*, *64*, 1369.

Fowler, A. (2020). Partisan intoxication or policy voting? *Quarterly Journal of Political Science*, *15*(2), 141–179.

Frohlich, N., & Oppenheimer, J. A. (1992). *Choosing justice: An experimental approach to ethical theory* (Vol. 22). University of California Press.

Frohlich, N., Oppenheimer, J. A., & Eavey, C. L. (1987). Laboratory results on Rawls's distributive justice. *British Journal of Political Science*, *17*(1), 1–21.

Furia, P. A. (2009). Democratic citizenship and the hypocrisy of leaders. *Polity*, *41*(1), 113–133.

Galston, W. A. (2017). *Anti-pluralism: The populist threat to liberal democracy*. Yale University Press.

Gerschewski, J. (2021). Explanations of institutional change: Reflecting on a "missing diagonal." *American Political Science Review*, *115*(1), 218–233.

Graham, M. H., & Svolik, M. W. (2020). Democracy in America? partisanship, polarization, and the robustness of support for democracy in the United States. *American Political Science Review*, *114*(2), 392–409. https://doi.org/10.1017/s0003055420000052.

Grofman, B., Koetzle, W., & Brunell, T. (1997). An integrated perspective on the three potential sources of partisan bias: Malapportionment, turnout differences, and the geographic distribution of party vote shares. *Electoral Studies*, *16*(4), 457–470.

Grossman, G., Kronick, D., Levendusky, M., & Meredith, M. (2022). The majoritarian threat to liberal democracy. *Journal of Experimental Political Science*, *9*(1), 36–45.

Grumbach, J. (2022). *Laboratories against democracy: How national parties transformed state politics* (Vol. 184). Princeton University Press.

Grumbach, J. M. (2023). Laboratories of democratic backsliding. *American Political Science Review*, *117*(3), 967–984.

Grzymala-Busse, A. (2017). Global populisms and their impact. *Slavic Review*, *76*(S1), S3–S8.

Guay, B., & Johnston, C. D. (2022). Ideological asymmetries and the determinants of politically motivated reasoning. *American Journal of Political Science, 66*(2), 285–301.

Gulzar, S. (2021). Who enters politics and why? *Annual Review of Political Science, 24*, 253–275.

Hacker, J. S., & Pierson, P. (2015). Confronting asymmetric polarization. *Solutions to Political Polarization in America, 59*, 66.

Haggard, S., & Kaufman, R. R. (2016). Democratization during the third wave. *Annual Review of Political Science, 19*, 125–144.

Hainmueller, J., & Hopkins, D. J. (2015, 07). The hidden American immigration consensus: A conjoint analysis of attitudes toward immigrants. *American Journal of Political Science, 59*(3), 529–548. https://doi.org/10.1111/ajps.12138.

Hall, A. B. (2019). *Who wants to run? How the devaluing of political office drives polarization*. University of Chicago Press.

Hawkins, K., & Littvay, L. (2019). *Contemporary US populism in comparative perspective*. Cambridge University Press.

Hicks, W. D., McKee, S. C., Sellers, M. D., & Smith, D. A. (2015). A principle or a strategy? voter identification laws and partisan competition in the American states. *Political Research Quarterly, 68*(1), 18–33.

Hicks, W. D., McKee, S. C., & Smith, D. A. (2016). The determinants of state legislator support for restrictive voter id laws. *State Politics & Policy Quarterly, 16*(4), 411–431.

Hicks, W. D., McKee, S. C., & Smith, D. A. (2021). Contemporary views of liberal democracy and the 2016 presidential election. *PS: Political Science & Politics, 54*(1), 33–40.

Higley, J., & Burton, M. G. (2006). *Elite foundations of liberal democracy*. Rowman & Littlefield.

Hofstadter, R. (1964). *Anti-intellectualism in American life*. Vintage.

Holliday, D. E., Iyengar, S., Lelkes, Y., & Westwood, S. J. (2024). Uncommon and nonpartisan: Antidemocratic attitudes in the American public. *Proceedings of the National Academy of Sciences, 121*(13), e2313013121.

Hopkins, D. J. (2018). *The increasingly United States: How and why American political behavior nationalized*. University of Chicago Press.

Houle, C., & Kenny, P. D. (2018). The political and economic consequences of populist rule in Latin America. *Government and Opposition, 53*(2), 256–287.

Howarth, D. (2014). *Ernesto Laclau: Post-Marxism, populism and critique*. Routledge.

Huber, R. A., & Schimpf, C. H. (2016). Friend or foe? testing the influence of populism on democratic quality in Latin America. *Political Studies*, *64*(4), 872–889.

Iyengar, S., Lelkes, Y., Levendusky, M., Malhotra, N., & Westwood, S. J. (2019). The origins and consequences of affective polarization in the United States. *Annual Review of Political Science*, *22*, 129–146.

Jacobson, G. C. (2021). Donald trump's big lie and the future of the republican party. *Presidential Studies Quarterly*, *51*(2), 273–289. https://onlinelibrary.wiley.com/doi/abs/10.1111/psq.12716. https://doi.org/10.1111/psq.12716.

Jerit, J., & Barabas, J. (2023). Are nonprobability surveys fit for purpose? *Public Opinion Quarterly*, *87*(3), 816–840.

Kalla, J. L., & Porter, E. (2021). Correcting bias in perceptions of public opinion among American elected officials: Results from two field experiments. *British Journal of Political Science*, *51*(4), 1792–1800.

Kenny, P. D. (2017). *Populism and patronage: Why populists win elections in India, Asia, and beyond*. Oxford University Press.

Kingzette, J., Druckman, J. N., Klar, S. et al. (2021). How affective polarization undermines support for democratic norms. *Public Opinion Quarterly*, *85*(2), 663–677. https://doi.org/10.1093/poq/nfab029.

Krishnarajan, S. (2023). Rationalizing democracy: The perceptual bias and (un) democratic behavior. *American Political Science Review*, *117*(2), 474–496.

Layman, G., Lee, F., & Wolbrecht, C. (2023). Political parties and loser's consent in American politics. *The ANNALS of the American Academy of Political and Social Science*, *708*(1), 164–183.

Lee, F. E. (2016). *Insecure majorities: Congress and the perpetual campaign*. University of Chicago Press.

Lee, F. E. (2020). Populism and the American party system: Opportunities and constraints. *Perspectives on Politics*, *18*(2), 370–388.

Lee, N. (2022). Do policy makers listen to experts? evidence from a national survey of local and state policy makers. *American Political Science Review*, *116*(2), 677–688.

Lee, N., Chen, K., Marble, W., & Bram, C. (2025). *Voice and value: How elected officials evaluate online and offline constituent feedback. Public Opinion Quarterly.* https://doi.org/10.1093/poq/nfaf006

Leeper, T. J., Hobolt, S. B., & Tilley, J. (2020). Measuring subgroup preferences in conjoint experiments. *Political Analysis*, *28*(2), 207–221.

Lees, J., & Cikara, M. (2020). Inaccurate group meta-perceptions drive negative out-group attributions in competitive contexts. *Nature Human Behaviour*, *4*(3), 279–286. https://doi.org/10.1038/s41562-019-0766-4.

Lenharo, M., & Wolf, L. (2024). Controversial virus-hunting scientist skewered at US covid-origins hearing. *Nature*.

Levendusky, M. (2009). *The partisan sort: How liberals became democrats and conservatives became republicans*. University of Chicago Press.

Levitsky, S., & Ziblatt, D. (2019). *How democracies die*. Crown.

MacInnis, B., Krosnick, J. A., Ho, A. S., & Cho, M.- J. (2018). The accuracy of measurements with probability and nonprobability survey samples: Replication and extension. *Public Opinion Quarterly*, *82*(4), 707–744.

Madison, J. (1787). The federalist no. 10. *November*, *22*(1787), 1787–1788.

Mangset, M., Engelstad, F., Teigen, M., & Gulbrandsen, T. (2019). The populist elite paradox: Using elite theory to elucidate the shapes and stakes of populist elite critiques. In Engelstad, F., Gulbrandsen, T., Mangset, M. and Teigen, M., eds., *Elites and people: Challenges to democracy* (Vol. 34, pp. 203–222). Emerald Publishing Limited.

Mansbridge, J., & Macedo, S. (2019). Populism and democratic theory. *Annual Review of Law and Social Science*, *15*(1), 59–77.

McClosky, H. (1964). Consensus and ideology in American politics. *American Political Science Review*, *58*(2), 361–382.

McClosky, H., & Brill, A. (1983). *The dimensions of tolerance: What Americans believe about civil liberties*. Russell Sage Foundation.

McClosky, H., Hoffmann, P. J., & O'Hara, R. (1960). Issue conflict and consensus among party leaders and followers. *American Political Science Review*, *54*(2), 406–427.

McClosky, H., & Zaller, J. (1984). *The American ethos: Public attitudes toward capitalism and democracy*. Harvard University Press.

McCoy, J., Rahman, T., & Somer, M. (2018). Polarization and the global crisis of democracy: Common patterns, dynamics, and pernicious consequences for democratic polities. *American Behavioral Scientist*, *62*(1), 16–42.

McGann, A. J. (2006). *The logic of democracy: Reconciling equality, deliberation, and minority protection*. University of Michigan Press.

Mernyk, J. S., Pink, S. L., Druckman, J. N., & Willer, R. (2022). Correcting inaccurate metaperceptions reduces Americans' support for partisan violence. *Proceedings of the National Academy of Sciences*, *119*(16), e2116851119.

Merrill, S., Grofman, B., & Brunell, T. (2022). Identifying the "downsian ceiling": When does polarization make appealing to one's base more attractive than moderating to the center. *Journal of Political Institutions and Political Economy*, *3*(3–4), 273–293. https://doi.org/ 10.1561/113.00000060.

Montgomery, J. M., Nyhan, B., & Torres, M. (2018). How conditioning on posttreatment variables can ruin your experiment and what to do about it. *American Journal of Political Science*, *62*(3), 760–775.

Moore-Berg, S. L., Ankori-Karlinsky, L.-O., Hameiri, B., & Bruneau, E. (2020). Exaggerated meta-perceptions predict intergroup hostility between American political partisans. *Proceedings of the National Academy of Sciences*, *117*(26), 14864–14872. https://doi.org/10.1073/pnas.2001263117.

Mounk, Y. (2018). *The people vs. democracy: Why our freedom is in danger and how to save it.* Harvard University Press.

Mudde, C. (2004). The populist zeitgeist. *Government and Opposition*, *39*(4), 541–563.

Mudde, C., & Kaltwasser, C. R. (2017). *Populism: A very short introduction.* Oxford University Press.

Mudde, C., & Rovira Kaltwasser, C. (2018). Studying populism in comparative perspective: Reflections on the contemporary and future research agenda. *Comparative Political Studies*, *51*(13), 1667–1693.

Müller, J.-W. (2017). *What is populism?* Penguin UK.

Müller, J.-W., & Ignatieff, M. (2018). How can populism be defeated? In Michael Ignatieff and Stefan Roch, eds., *Rethinking Open Society*, 195–210. Budapest: Central European University Press. https://doi.org/10.1515/9789633862711-016

Mullin, M., & Hansen, K. (2023). Local news and the electoral incentive to invest in infrastructure. *American Political Science Review*, *117*(3), 1145–1150.

Mullinix, K. J., Leeper, T. J., Druckman, J. N., & Freese, J. (2015). The generalizability of survey experiments. *Journal of Experimental Political Science*, *2*(2), 109–138.

Nichols, T. (2017). *The death of expertise: The campaign against established knowledge and why it matters*. Oxford University Press.

Ober, J. (1989). *The nature of Athenian democracy.* University of Chicago Press.

Oliver, J. E., & Rahn, W. M. (2016). Rise of the trumpenvolk: Populism in the 2016 election. *The ANNALS of the American Academy of Political and Social Science*, *667*(1), 189–206.

Osborne, M. J., & Slivinski, A. (1996). A model of political competition with citizen-candidates. *The Quarterly Journal of Economics*, *111*(1), 65–96.

Peffley, M., & Rohrschneider, R. (2007, 08). Elite Beliefs and the Theory of Democratic Elitism. In *The Oxford handbook of political behavior*. Oxford University Press. https://doi.org/10.1093/oxfordhb/9780199270125.003.0004.

Piano, N. (2019). Revisiting democratic elitism: The Italian school of elitism, American political science, and the problem of plutocracy. *The Journal of Politics*, *81*(2), 524–538.

Pierson, P., & Schickler, E. (2020). Madison's constitution under stress: A developmental analysis of political polarization. *Annual Review of Political Science*, *23*, 37–58.

Prothro, J. W., & Grigg, C. M. (1960). Fundamental principles of democracy: Bases of agreement and disagreement. *The Journal of Politics*, *22*(2), 276–294.

Riker, W. H. (1988). *Liberalism against populism: A confrontation between the theory of democracy and the theory of social choice*. Waveland Press.

Rooduijn, M., & Pauwels, T. (2011). Measuring populism: Comparing two methods of content analysis. *West European Politics*, *34*(6), 1272–1283.

Ruth, S. P. (2018). Populism and the erosion of horizontal accountability in Latin America. *Political Studies*, *66*(2), 356–375.

Scheppele, K. L. (2018). Autocratic legalism. *The University of Chicago Law Review*, *85*(2), 545–584.

Schubert, L., Dye, T. R., & Zeigler, H. (2015). *The irony of democracy: An uncommon introduction to American politics*. Cengage Learning.

Shaffer, R., Pinson, L. E., Chu, J. A., & Simmons, B. A. (2020). Local elected officials' receptivity to refugee resettlement in the United States. *Proceedings of the National Academy of Sciences*, *117*(50), 31722–31728.

Shor, B. & McCarty, N. (2022). Two decades of polarization in American state legislatures. *Journal of Political Institutions and Political Economy*, *3*(3–4), 343–370.

Simonovits, G., McCoy, J., & Littvay, L. (2022). Democratic hypocrisy and out-group threat: Explaining citizen support for democratic erosion. *The Journal of Politics*, *84*(3), 1806–1811.

Sniderman, P. M., Fletcher, J. F., Russel, P. H., Tetlock, P. E., & Prior, M. (2000). The theory of democratic elitism revisited: A response to Vengroff and Morton. *Canadian Journal of Political Science/Revue canadienne de science politique*, *33*(3), 569–586.

Sniderman, P. M., Fletcher, J. F., Russell, P. H., Tetlock, P. E., & Gaines, B. J. (1991). The fallacy of democratic elitism: Elite competition and commitment to civil liberties. *British Journal of Political Science*, *21*(3), 349–370.

Sniderman, P. M., Fletcher, J. F., Tetlock, P. E., & Russell, P. H. (1996). *The clash of rights: Liberty, equality, and legitimacy in pluralist democracy*. Yale University Press.

Sullivan, J. L., Walsh, P., Shamir, M., Barnum, D. G., & Gibson, J. L. (1993). Why politicians are more tolerant: Selective recruitment and socialization among political elites in Britain, Israel, New Zealand and the United States. *British Journal of Political Science*, *23*(1), 51–76.

Taggart, P. (2018). Populism and "unpolitics." In Fitzi, G., Mackert, J. and Turner, B, eds., *Populism and the crisis of democracy* (pp. 79–87). Routledge.

Thompson, G. F. (2017). Populisms and liberal democracy–business as usual? *Economy and Society*, *46*(1), 43–59.

Thomsen, D. M. (2014). Ideological moderates won't run: How party fit matters for partisan polarization in congress. *The Journal of Politics*, *76*(3), 786–797.

Thomsen, D. M. (2017). *Opting out of congress: Partisan polarization and the decline of moderate candidates*. Cambridge University Press.

Todd, J. D., Bram, C., & Krishnamurthy, A. (2024). Do at-large elections reduce black representation? a new baseline for county legislatures. *Electoral Studies*, *88*, 102750.

Urbinati, N. (2019). *Me the people: How populism transforms democracy*. Harvard University Press.

Uslaner, E. M. (1991). Comity in context: Confrontation in historical perspective. *British Journal of Political Science*, *21*(1), 45–77.

Uslaner, E. M. (1993). *The decline of comity in congress*. University of Michigan Press.

Vachudova, M. A. (2021). Populism, democracy, and party system change in Europe. *Annual Review of Political Science*, *24*, 471–498.

Voelkel, J. G., Chu, J., Stagnaro, M. N. et al. (2023). Interventions reducing affective polarization do not necessarily improve anti-democratic attitudes. *Nature Human Behaviour*, *7*(1), 55–64.

Waldner, D., & Lust, E. (2018). Unwelcome change: Coming to terms with democratic backsliding. *Annual Review of Political Science*, *21*, 93–113.

Westfall, J., Van Boven, L., Chambers, J. R., & Judd, C. M. (2015). Perceiving political polarization in the United States: Party identity strength and attitude extremity exacerbate the perceived partisan divide. *Perspectives on Psychological Science*, *10*(2), 145–158.

Wunsch, N., & Gessler, T. (2023). Who tolerates democratic backsliding? a mosaic approach to voters' responses to authoritarian leadership in Hungary. *Democratization*, *30*(5), 914–937. https://doi.org/10.1080/13510347.2023.2203918.

Zaller, J., & Feldman, S. (1992). A simple theory of the survey response: Answering questions versus revealing preferences. *American Journal of Political Science*, *36*(3), 579–616.

Zürn, M. (2022). How non-majoritarian institutions make silent majorities vocal: A political explanation of authoritarian populism. *Perspectives on Politics*, *20*(3), 788–807.

Acknowledgments

For help with this project, I am especially grateful to Jamie Druckman. I also thank John Aldrich, Fani Bram, Tom Brunell, Siv Cheruvu, Rebecca Cordell, James Cragun, Jared Edgerton, Anthony Fowler, James Harrington, Chris Johnston, Arvind Krishnamurthy, Nathan Lee, Katherine McCabe, Charles Nathan, Lauren Ratliff Santoro, Marianne Stewart, and Jason Todd. Funding for the first three studies was provided by the Worldview Lab at the Kenan Institute for Ethics at Duke University. Funding for the fourth and fifth studies was provided by The University of Texas at Dallas. I thank the Institute for Humane Studies (grant #: IHS017901) for their support in publishing this Element open access. Finally, I am grateful to Wioletta Dziuda, Anthony Fowler, and William Howell for inviting me on the *Not Another Politics Podcast* to discuss this project.

Cambridge Elements

Experimental Political Science

James N. Druckman
University of Rochester

James N. Druckman is the Martin Brewer Anderson Professor of Political Science at the University of Rochester. He served as an editor for the journals Political Psychology and Public Opinion Quarterly as well as the University of Chicago Press's series in American Politics. He currently is the co-Principal Investigator of Time-sharing Experiments for the Social Sciences (TESS) and sits on the boards of the American National Election Studies, the General Social Survey, and the Russell Sage Foundation. He previously served as President of the American Political Science Association section on Experimental Research and helped oversee the launching of the Journal of Experimental Political Science. He was co-editor of the Cambridge Handbook of Experimental Political Science and Advances in Experimental Political Science. He authored the book Experimental Thinking: A Primer on Social Science Experiments. He is a Fellow of the American Academy of Arts and Sciences and has published approximately 200 articles/book chapters on public opinion, political communication, campaigns, research methods, and other topics.

About the Series

There currently are few outlets for extended works on experimental methodology in political science. The new Experimental Political Science Cambridge Elements series features research on experimental approaches to a given substantive topic, and experimental methods by prominent and upcoming experts in the field.

Cambridge Elements

Experimental Political Science

Elements in the Series

A full series listing is available at: www.cambridge.org/EXPS

For EU product safety concerns, contact us at Calle de José Abascal, 56–1°, 28003 Madrid, Spain or eugpsr@cambridge.org.

www.ingramcontent.com/pod-product-compliance
Ingram Content Group UK Ltd.
Pitfield, Milton Keynes, MK11 3LW, UK
UKHW020422250726
13967UKWH00007B/2769

* 9 7 8 1 0 0 9 5 4 6 9 4 2 *